teach®
yourself

mahjong

teach®
yourself

mahjong
david pritchard

The **teach yourself** series does exactly what it says, and it works. For over 60 years, more than 40 million people have learnt over 750 subjects the **teach yourself** way, with impressive results.

be where you want to be
with **teach yourself**

For UK order enquiries: please contact Bookpoint Ltd., 130 Milton Park, Abingdon, Oxon OX14 4SB. Telephone: +44 (0) 1235 827720. Fax: +44 (0) 1235 400454. Lines are open 09.00–18.00, Monday to Saturday, with a 24-hour message answering service. You can also order through our website www.madaboutbooks.com.

For USA order enquiries: please contact McGraw-Hill Customer Services, PO Box 545, Blacklick, OH 43004-0545, USA. Telephone: 1-800-722-4726. Fax: 1-614-755-5645.

For Canada order enquiries: please contact McGraw-Hill Ryerson Ltd., 300 Water St, Whitby, Ontario L1N 9B6, Canada. Telephone: 905 430 5000. Fax: 905 430 5020.

Long renowned as the authoritative source for self-guided learning – with more than 30 million copies sold worldwide – the *Teach Yourself* series includes over 300 titles in the fields of languages, crafts, hobbies, business, computing and education.

British Library Cataloguing in Publication Data: a catalogue entry for this title is available from The British Library

Library of Congress Catalog Card Number: On file

First published in UK 2001 by Hodder Headline Ltd., 338 Euston Road, London NW1 3BH.

First published in US 2001 by Contemporary Books, a Division of the McGraw Hill Companies, 1, Prudential Plaza, 130 East Randolph Street, Chicago, IL 60601 USA.

The 'Teach Yourself' name and logo are registered trade marks of Hodder & Stoughton Ltd.

Copyright © 2001, 2003 David Pritchard

Typeset by Transet Limited, Coventry, England.
Printed in Great Britain for Hodder & Stoughton Educational, a division of Hodder Headline Ltd, 338 Euston Road, London NW1 3BH by Cox & Wyman Ltd, Reading, Berkshire.

Impression number   10 9 8 7 6 5 4 3 2 1
Year   2009 2008 2007 2006 2005 2004 2003

contents

For Graham, Caroline and Jonathan, whose 7 a.m. game of mahjong has long been an institution.

introduction

The first impression many people have of mahjong is of a game of mysterious ritual and inscrutable rules. The illusion is quickly shattered with familiarity. Mahjong, the Game of the Four Winds, also called Sparrow, is a game for everyone. Its attraction is across the spectrum from young children to serious-minded adults. Mahjong is easy to learn and a pleasure to play although, like many other table games, mastery comes only after long experience. The visual appeal of mahjong, with its exotic designs and euphonious jargon, cannot be disputed, and there is also a seductive pleasure in the manipulation of the tiles. Anyone who has travelled in the East will be familiar with the relentless clicking emanating from house after house in street after street. Many are captivated by the game's oriental trappings, not all of which, it must be admitted, originated in the East. But perhaps the most pleasing, if least obvious, feature of the game is its simplicity.

Mahjong has many similarities with the card game rummy and if you know how to play rummy you already know half the rules of mahjong. But the similarities are deceptive, for at heart the games are very different. In mahjong players compete as individuals so the game mercifully lacks the recriminations common to partnership games. Also a weak mahjong hand can be quickly transformed into a good one, thus sustaining the interest. Add to this the sense of anticipation that persists throughout the game, and it is hardly surprising that many people find it highly addictive. Chance plays a large element in mahjong so it goes almost without saying that winning should be treated with modesty and failure without guilt or regret.

Mahjong originated in China about a century ago but like other games whose origins are obscure, many absurd claims have been made for its antiquity. In its homeland it is arguably a national pastime not totally unconnected with the oriental passion for gambling. (Mahjong soon replaced Fan Tan in the gambling houses.) It is also immensely popular in those countries with cultural links to China as well as, predictably, amongst Chinese communities everywhere.

You may have come across mahjong under another name —R. F. Foster, a leading authority on the game, listed 21 of these. In large part this is due to the many Chinese dialects and to a lesser extent to Western businessmen who early on sought to trademark the sets they imported. The different names for the game however are no more than academic. What really matters are the rules and here also there is division. A writer recently appealed 'Will the real Mah Jong rules please stand up?'. Alas, there are no 'real rules' to stand up for they largely depend on where you live and who you play with. There is a joke going the rounds in China that Taiwan will never be reunited with the motherland because they will not be able to agree on the rules of mahjong. The game described here however is the original game as played in China in the early years of the last century and described in detail by A. D. Millington in his authoritative work *The Complete Book of Mah-Jongg* (1977).

The many variations on the original game can be attributed to the lack of an international authority to codify the rules. But the diversity of rules is perhaps something of the game's charm for it offers a selection of variant games that appeal to different tastes. The two main branches are American and Japanese mahjong, both described later although here again there are variants, as indeed there are in the Chinese game. In China there is little conformity, despite an attempt to impose a uniform structure, as the rules are commonly passed by word of mouth from generation to generation. However, it will comfort you to know that the differences between the various forms of the game are confined to details.

In the East the sexes are usually segregated by choice. The game is not widely played in Europe, at least in an organized form, but in America, where it is estimated that there are a third of a million regular players, mahjong is overwhelmingly played by women. The West quickly took to mahjong. A craze for the game hit Britain in the early- to mid-1920s, a craze that has probably never been equalled by any game before or since. *The Times* ran leaders couched in mahjong terms, the chief barman of the Savoy created a mahjong cocktail for his customers, and instruction books rolled off the presses in profusion. But perhaps the most dramatic evidence of the popularity of the game is that in 1923 mahjong sets outsold radios (then called wirelesses) in Britain although they were in the same price range and the radio was the principal source of home entertainment at the time. Interest in the game then fell away with the introduction of contract bridge but perhaps more particularly because of the many embellishments that were added to the rules at that time causing confusion and eventually disillusion. One of the reasons for the divergence of rules in the West, and particularly in America, was the argument that the origins of mahjong were based on an alien and little-understood psychology and needed adjustment to Western ways to satisfy the market. In the transformation, unfortunately, the inner harmony of the Chinese game was largely lost.

You are of course free to choose which rules you please, subject, one supposes, to the agreement of your playing partners. You can stay with the Chinese game or elect to play one or other of the versions described later. Indeed, there is nothing to stop you introducing what are called 'table rules', homespun amendments that take your fancy. In particular, I would recommend that if you are engaged in a purely social game you relax the penalties for rule infringements.

Sooner or later you may want to buy a mahjong set. The purchase will be a once-in-a-lifetime expense as even with ordinary care a modern set is likely to outlast its owner. Choice is a matter of personal taste. Mahjong sets have always tended to vary slightly from manufacturer to manufacturer, both in design and sometimes in content, so it is worth shopping around for a set that pleases you. Modern sets today are commonly of acrylic or plastic but they can vary considerably from relatively cheap sets of basic design and lurid colours to those of more intricate design and of superior quality. Plastic tiles have the advantage of being of uniform colour and easy to clean. If you can afford one, an antique set carved in ivory or bone by an individual craftsman and backed by bamboo may tempt you and can be a source of lasting pleasure. These early mahjong sets, still commonly found in auctions, were often sold in cabinets, lacquered in the Chinese style. But both bone and ivory discolour with time and in addition old sets may contain chipped tiles. Be warned: sharp players can turn these imperfections to their advantage! If on the other hand you consider a mahjong set an unwarranted expense there is fortunately a much cheaper alternative – mahjong cards.

The game in Britain remains largely confined to the family or social circle. There are few clubs where mahjong is played and these tend to have a short life. But you need not lack opponents as there are many sites on the Internet devoted to the game (the chapter on American Mahjong lists a few) and if you cannot make up a four at home (the ideal number) there is a good choice of software opponents. You can even buy an electronic set to reduce your labours, although these are not very popular as they eliminate the sound of the tiles, an aural pleasure for most players.

I am heavily indebted to Peter Blommers for his meticulous proof-reading and wise advice. To 'blommerize' a manuscript is a verb known to several authors.

01

the mahjong set

In this chapter you will learn:
- the mahjong tiles
- about scoring sticks and their markings
- about useful accessories.

A mahjong set comprises a basic set of 136 tiles that are common to all variations of the game. A set may, and probably will, also include bonus tiles and/or jokers. These are liable to vary from country to country and even from manufacturer to manufacturer, both in content and design. There are also a few accessories which may or may not be included with the set.

Modern sets are usually of plastic. Plastic tiles have the advantage of being relatively cheap. Even with modest care, a set will last a lifetime. Early mahjong sets were often sold in handsome mahogany or rosewood cabinets. The tiles were of ivory or bone, sometimes of wood, all of which tended to discolour with time. The ivory and bone sets were often dovetailed into a bamboo back. These old sets are today collectors' items and command good prices in fine condition.

Mahjong tiles, sometimes called cards or bricks, measure approximately 30 mm × 23 mm × 15 mm. Tile designs tend to be in primary colours, usually blue or black, green and red, on a white background. The reverse of the tiles, similar to the reverse of playing cards, is uniform, and is often of bamboo or coloured plastic.

The basic set

The basic set is made up of three suits, each of nine different tiles. In addition there are two sets of honour tiles, one of four designs, the other of three, a total of 34 distinct tiles. There are four identical tiles of each design making a total of 136 tiles.

The three **suits** are **bamboos**, **characters** and **circles**. They correspond approximately to the suits in playing cards. In sets destined for the Western market they carry Arabic numerals to assist in identification; an innovation claimed for **Joseph Babcock** who took the game to America, but more likely the inspiration of an unknown benefactor who introduced the indices for the benefit of players in expatriate clubs in the foreign concessions and treaty ports of China, and particularly Shanghai, around the turn of the twentieth century. The numerals are omitted on Chinese sets. Mahjong, like most games that have achieved a wide popularity, has predictably acquired a vocabulary of slang expressions.

Bamboo tiles are numbered from 1 to 9. The 1 of bamboos is a curiosity. It is usually represented by a sparrow or rice-bird, or rarely some other bird, but it can also be a bamboo shoot which looks a bit like a pineapple. The 1 of bamboos, commonly known as the Cocky-Olly bird, although no-one seems to know why, is easily confused with one or other of the bonus tiles (see below). The 2s are used as jokers by some players but this is not recommended. The 6 can be mistaken for a 9 by the unwary, and vice versa. The 8 of bamboos is familiarly known as 'gates'. Examine the tile and you will see why. The bamboo sticks on the 2, 3, 4, 6 and 8 tiles are uniquely coloured green. The other values, (5, 7, 9), apart from the 1 of bamboos, which is normally multicoloured, have one or more bamboo sticks in red and are therefore sometimes known as 'red bamboos'. The colours have implications for the game. The suit is sometimes referred to as 'sticks', 'boos' or 'bams'.

Circle tiles are numbered from 1 to 9. In popular parlance, the suit is called by a number of names: balls, buttons, cakes, cash, coins, dots and rings (take your pick!). The 1 of circles is known as the 'Moon of China', or more vulgarly as 'soup plate'. The 8 of circles is similarly known as the 'dinner service'. The 2 of circles is the 'snake's eyes'.

Character tiles are numbered from 1 to 9. The upper ideographs are the Chinese numbers from 1 to 9; the lower ideograph, common to all the character tiles, is the Chinese word 'won' or 'wan', meaning 'myriad' or '10 000'. Thus the 7 of characters, for example, is '70 000'. If a Chinese set (without indices) is in use, it is important to recognize the different numbers. The suit is sometimes known as cracks or actors. The 8 of characters is familiarly called the 'high jump'.

The 2s to 8s of each suit are known as **simples**:

Although simples are numbered, they have no ranking so, for example, a 2 of bamboos is equal in all respects to an 8 of circles.

The 1s and 9s of each suit are known as **terminals**. They are sometimes called the 'old head' tiles. The 1s and 9s are of equal value.

The dragons and the winds are known as **honour** tiles. There are four of each denomination.

There are three **dragons**: green, red and white. They are all of equal value.

The green and red dragons display Chinese ideographs. These tiles are easy to distinguish as they are invariably coloured green and red, respectively. The green dragon is associated with the East and is sometimes called a phoenix. It is referred to flippantly as 'spinach'. The white dragon is normally a blank tile (as above) but in some sets it is shown with a frame:

In some sets too the dragon tiles also carry roman letter indices:

Red dragon = C (chung), meaning centre or middle, reflecting the traditional Chinese concept of China being at the centre of the world — the Middle Kingdom. The Chinese recognize five directions: the cardinal points and the centre from which they radiate.
Green dragon = F (fa) meaning green.
White dragon = P (pai) meaning pure.

The red, green and white dragons represent, according to some sources, animal, plant and spiritual life, respectively; whilst another interpretation has the dragons representing the three virtues expounded by Confucius: benevolence, sincerity and filial piety. None of these relationships, you will be glad to know, has any relevance for the game. However, the dragons are sometimes associated with the suits: the red dragon with characters, the green dragon with bamboos and the white dragon with circles.

There are four **wind** or direction tiles; East, South, West and North. These are almost invariably coloured blue or black. Each tile carries the Chinese ideograph for the direction. Roman letters identify the tiles in sets produced for Western markets. As with the Arabic numerals on the suits, these are omitted in indigenous sets. The winds are theoretically all of equal value but individual winds enjoy certain bonuses in play. In another bit of symbolism, the four winds and the red dragon (the centre) are said to represent the five elements; wood, fire, earth, metal and water.

The honour tiles (winds and dragons), together with the terminals (1s and 9s of each suit), are collectively known as **major tiles** and have implications for scoring.

The simples (the 2s to 8s of each suit) are known as **minor tiles**.

The **lucky tiles** are the dragons, the prevailing wind and the player's wind (see below) so they vary with the player. They are called lucky tiles, especially in the United States, because they can earn extra points.

Here is the complete basic set of 136 tiles:

Supplementary tiles

Most mahjong sets include two sets of four **bonus tiles** commonly referred to as **flowers** and **seasons**. These **supplementary** tiles are exactly that — bonus tiles. They score points for their fortunate owners but in no way affect the play. They are not used in some countries, and are often omitted between strong players, as they increase the chance element and hence reduce the skill of the game.

Bonus tiles come in a bewildering number of designs as they offer the engravers the chance to demonstrate their skills. (Sets of bonus tiles featuring nymphs scattering flowers, Chinese classical drama and travel scenes are recorded, but these are rarities.) In the more expensive sets the designs on flower and season tiles can be highly artistic, almost miniature works of art; in cheap sets on the other hand the designs are fairly basic. There are four tiles in each of the two sets, numbered from 1 to 4; one set, usually flowers, commonly numbered in red, the other in blue, green or black. Sometimes the season tiles carry the numbers in Chinese. This should pose no problems as the numbers correspond to those at the top of the character tiles 1–4. Bonus tiles are proper to the winds as follows: 1, east wind; 2, south wind; 3, west wind; 4, north wind. These relationships have implications for the game. It is important to note that there is only one of each bonus tile in contrast to the four of each tile in the basic set. A complete set of four bonus tiles (either flowers or seasons) is called a **bouquet**. Sometimes both sets are simply referred to as 'flowers'.

The **seasons** are predictable: (1–4) **Spring, Summer, Autumn** and **Winter**. Designs reflect the seasons as interpreted by the craftsman and can vary enormously.

Flowers, in contrast, are far from predictable but the traditional Chinese flowers as commonly shown are, respectively (1–4), **plum blossom, orchid, chrysanthemum** and **bamboo**. However, other subjects are not infrequent:

Many sets, particularly those destined for the American market, are now sold with four or eight **jokers**. These tiles usually have a single design, for example a goose or a horse, but many carry different designs in bewildering array: cat, rat, cock, worm, old man, snow, moon and bag of gold are just a few. Jokers are not used in the Chinese and Japanese games, nor are they normally included in European sets.

Most sets include four blank tiles:

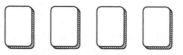

These are spares intended to replace any tiles that are lost or damaged. A felt pen can be used to mark a replacement tile. In China, one could take the tile to the local mahjong dealer and have it engraved for a modest charge. Spare tiles, sometimes used as jokers, should not be confused with white dragons. In many sets the two are identical. Where this occurs it is advisable to ring the changes so that the tiles endure the same wear.

Accessories

Accessories are useful aids for play but not essential for the game.

Scoring sticks, known as **tallies**, **chips** or **bones**, are often included with a mahjong set. Except in modern sets bought in the Far East, tallies are in four values. These carry markings in contrasting colours, often crude, and have the following values, illogical to Western eyes:

1 red and 3 black spots: 2 points
8 black or red spots: 10 points
2 red spots: 100 points
6 black and 6 red spots: 500 points

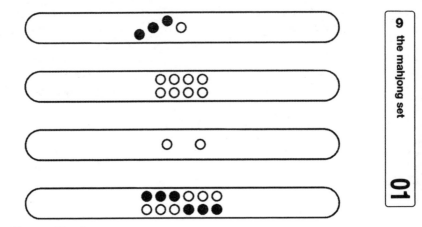

tallies — old style

Better-quality tallies tend to have the same markings, but at both ends:

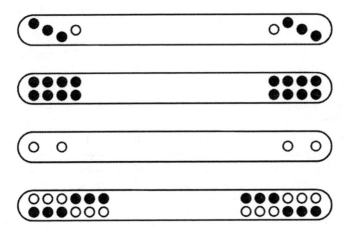

end markings — old style

In many sets intended for Western markets, the values are the same as in the old style but the markings correspond more closely with the values.

2 black spots: 2 points
10 black spots: 10 points
1 red spot: 100 points
5 red spots: 500 points

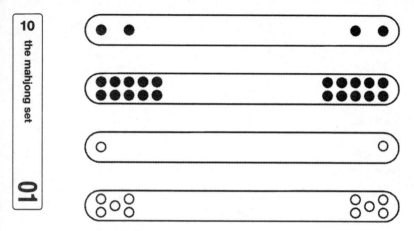

modern-style tallies

In sets sold today in China and Hong Kong, and rarely exported, there are only three values, represented by counters without markings but in contrasting colours: 12 in one colour, 16 in another and 40 in a third colour. These are compatible with the radical scoring system of **faans** and **laaks** introduced to the native game in the last few decades. Other types of tallies are rarely met.

A **wind indicator** is usually included in a set. This may take the form of a rotating disc in which the prevailing wind is shown in the window:

wind disc showing prevailing wind

An alternative is a small box, the **chuang-tzu**, also known as the tong or jong (dealer) box, which contains four wind counters, shown below, and serves the same purpose as the wind disc. Notice that the directions are not in the conventional sequence North, South, East and West. This will be explained later.

wind counters
left to right: East, South, West, North

A set usually includes three or four small cubic **dice,** although only two are used in the game. The numbers 1 and 4 on the dice are invariably in red, an auspicious colour for the Chinese; the other four numbers are in black.

Racks for holding the players' hands are a useful accessory. They have a secondary use as rulers. Racks are almost invariably sold separately. Racks are the same length as the sides of the walls (building walls is a necessary preliminary of the game, as will be seen). The Chinese, incidentally, scorn racks: they either stand the tiles upright on the table in front of them or hold them in their hand.

Rulers (four, if included in a set) are commonly the length of 17 tiles and are used for evening up the tiles in a line in the preliminary stage. Rulers are a luxury and are unnecessary if racks are used since they can serve the same purpose.

02

preliminaries

In this chapter you will learn:
- who sits where
- preparations for play
- how the tiles are distributed.

Preparations for play divide into three stages: seating, building the wall and the deal. These may appear over-elaborate but they were formulated to minimize the opportunities for cheating (mahjong was much used for gambling).

Seating

Seats in mahjong are designated by the four cardinal points, East, South, West and North, and by extension the players are referred to as East, South, West and North. It is important to note that directions do not correspond with conventional compass directions: the positions of North and South or East and West are reversed. This is because for the Chinese they are projected onto heaven (look at them upside down). The seating is like this:

the seating

Importance of East

East, who is sometimes called the dealer, leader or **jong**, is always the dominant wind, as befits a game coming from China. The main reason for the importance of East is that he pays or receives double in the post-game reckoning. This in turn affects the play as East, with most to gain and most to lose, will likely have different priorities to the other players.

Allocation of seats

Seating is important as it has bearing on the scoring and hence the play. The formal procedure for determining who sits where, described below, is rather elaborate, but for social play any simple system will do. Two popular methods involve mixing one each of the four wind tiles face down, the players drawing to determine seating; the other method is for each player to roll two dice and total the scores, the highest total occupying the East seat, next highest the South seat, and so on (roll again to resolve ties).

The proper procedure is for the four players to sit at random round the table. One player casts two dice. These are totalled and the player then counts round the table in an anticlockwise direction in the Chinese manner, starting with self as 1. Thus a roll of 5 : 2 (total seven) would indicate the player opposite. The nominated player is temporary (or provisional) East and the other players are named successively temporary South, temporary West and temporary North anticlockwise from East. Temporary East now takes one of each of the wind tiles, shuffles them face down and arranges them in a row. At one end is placed any odd-numbered suit tile and at the other end any even-numbered suit tile. The arrangement looks like this:

arrangement of tiles to determine seating

The player who is temporary East (A) now casts the two dice and counts round the table anticlockwise, starting with self, as before. Supposing the dice show 5 : 1. This totals six, indicating temporary South (B).

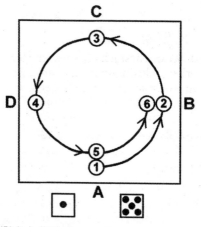

temporary South (B) is indicated

Because the dice total an even number, South picks up the wind tile adjacent to the even-numbered suit tile. Proceeding anticlockwise round the table, the players in turn take the next tile in line; so West takes the tile that was adjacent to the tile South picked, North takes the next tile and East the remaining tile adjacent to the odd-numbered suit tile. The tiles are exposed and determine the seating for the first round. The new East takes over from temporary East and the other players likewise assume their new identities. The player who drew the East tile does not move; the other players change seats as appropriate.

Mixing the tiles

All the tiles are now placed face down on the table and thoroughly shuffled. Usually the tiles are kept face up in their box on cardboard trays or similar. The easy way to avoid the tedium of turning the tiles over individually is to lay a book on top of a tray, hold the two firmly together, invert them and slide the tiles, which are now face down, onto the table.

Shuffling the tiles is inevitably noisy and is picturesquely known as the **'twittering of the sparrows'** or **'washing'**. In some circles East does not take part in this action. When all players agree that the tiles have been adequately mixed each player starts to build a wall.

Building the walls

Each player builds a **wall** 18 tiles long and two tiles high. If bonus tiles are omitted, each player builds a wall 17 tiles long (if only four bonus tiles are used, North and South build 17 **stacks**, East and West 18 stacks). Tiles are placed lengthwise against one another. Throughout this procedure tiles remain face down and must under no circumstances be examined. If a tile is turned over by accident it should be shuffled before continuing.

a player's completed wall

When all the players are ready they push their walls together to form a square. Racks or rulers are commonly used for this purpose to ensure alignment. The walls form a hollow square. By tradition, the right-hand side of each player's wall abuts the inside of the wall of the player to the right while the left-hand side defines the corner of the wall. This should be clear from the diagram. The walls together form, figuratively speaking, the walls of a city, often called, inappropriately, the **Great Wall of China**. The walls should fit flush together as superstition has it that any gap will allow evil spirits to enter and disrupt the game. The large square space between the walls is sometimes called the **courtyard**.

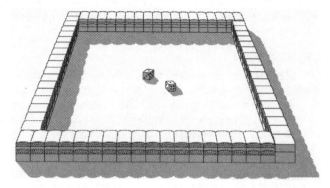

the completed square

Breaking the wall

East now takes the two dice and throws them within the walls and again totals them. Supposing the dice show 5 : 3, a total of eight. East counts round the players anticlockwise, starting with self, as before. The designated player is North (see diagram).

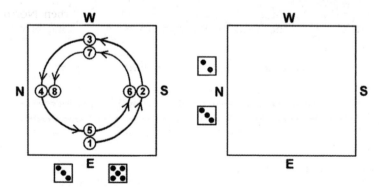

north is indicated (left) and rolls both dice again (right) to determine where the wall will be broken

North now throws the dice and adds them to East's roll. Supposing North rolls 3 : 2, a total of five, which when added to East's roll sums to 13. North now counts 13 stacks along his wall, starting at the end stack on the right and moving clockwise (i.e., along the wall to the left). On reaching the 13th stack, he removes it and places the two tiles on top of the wall as shown in the diagram below; the first (top) tile being placed a little further along the wall than the second (lower) tile. These tiles are known as **loose tiles** and are said to be 'on the roof'. Their precise placing is not important. Another break in the wall is then made 16 tiles (including the loose tiles) to the right of the first break, this time by simply separating the adjacent stacks by a discernible gap.

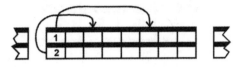

North's wall indicating breaks

This separated group of seven stacks and two loose tiles is known as the **kong box**, dead wall or golden wall and will be explained later. In fact, the second break is arbitrary (some players allocate 14 tiles to the kong box) and does not affect the game in any way. The **live wall** starts to the immediate left of the first break and ends at the right of the second break, i.e. at the 17th tile to the right of the first break. Should the combined dice rolls sum to more than 18, North would simply continue counting round the corner along West's wall before making the initial break. Should they sum to less than seven, then North would make the break to the right to form the kong box in East's wall.

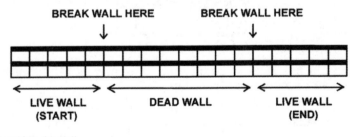

breaking the wall

The deal

Each player, starting with East and proceeding anticlockwise, now takes two stacks of tiles from the start of the live wall immediately to the left of the first break, and places them, faces facing, on his rack. Players should conceal their tiles from the other players. The start of the wall, showing the tiles taken by East and South, is illustrated in the diagram below.

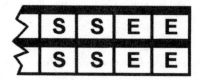

the deal

This action is repeated three times, turning corners as necessary, when each player will have 12 tiles. A total of 48 tiles have now been removed from the wall. Recalling that North broke the wall between his 13th and 14th tile and the 48 tiles were removed in a clockwise direction, the next stack on the live wall will be the second stack in South's wall, counting from the right. East now takes the top tile of this stack, South takes the bottom tile, West takes the next top tile, North the bottom tile and East finally takes the top tile of the third stack (see the following diagram).

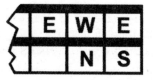

drawing of final tiles

East now has 14 tiles and the other three players 13 tiles each. The game proper is ready to start.

A **game** of mahjong is strictly made up of four **rounds**, each round named after a wind, called the prevailing wind or the wind of the round, and consisting of at least four hands. Amongst beginners a game may take several hours. A shorter game, for example a round, can be agreed instead.

A **hand** starts with the deal and ends when one player goes mahjong. A hand also ends if the live wall is exhausted before any player goes mahjong. This is a **draw** or **wash-out**. In the Chinese game, as described here, the last 14 tiles are not used and so are effectively dead. The 14 include any remaining in the kong box. Conversely, if the kong box was exhausted (very unlikely but possible), then replacement tiles during the game would be drawn from the end of the live wall. In either event the initial break at the end of the kong box would be ignored when counting the remaining tiles. After each hand the tiles are shuffled and the wall rebuilt and broken as before.

East is dealer for the first hand of the round and the jong disc is placed by East to indicate this. If East wins the hand or the hand is a draw, East retains the deal. When one of the other players goes mahjong or declares a special hand, which is the equivalent of going mahjong, the deal passes to the right. South now becomes the new East, West the new South, North the new West and East the new North. When each player has been East in turn the deal returns to the original East and the next round begins.

Here is an example of an average hand, based on probability. In practice of course no-one is dealt an average hand; however, it is not a bad idea to credit your opponents with a distribution like this as a starting point for your assessment of their hands.

Notice that the hand is made up of three tiles of each suit, two winds, a dragon and a bonus tile.

The first round is the east round. When (original) North loses his deal after four or more hands have been played, a round has been completed. At the end of a round, (original) East becomes dealer again. The second round is the South round. The only difference between this and the first round of play is that South is now the prevailing wind. When four rounds have been completed, that is, when each of the four winds has been prevailing wind for a round, the game is at an end.

Notice that, whereas play is anticlockwise, the wall is dismantled in a clockwise direction.

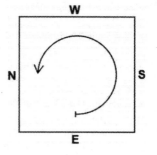

direction of play

At this stage, or before building the walls, tallies are distributed and a **limit** agreed. The limit is normally 500, 1000 (recommended) or 2000 points. If the limit is set at 1000 points, a sensible initial allocation to each player would be 2000 points distributed as 10 × 2 points; 8 × 10 points; 9 × 100 points and 2 × 500 points. However, there is nothing obligatory about this: players may agree on any limit and any values and distribution of tallies. Alternatively, scores could be kept on paper.

Because in theory, though very rarely in practice, near-astronomical scores can be reached, the limit agreed means that any score above it is ignored for settlement purposes. The limit is also a useful benchmark for special hands.

playing the game

In this chapter you will learn:
- how tiles are combined
- what constitutes a mahjong hand
- the play sequence
- the goulash.

Know your tiles

Before you start to play take time to familiarize yourself with the tiles. This is important if only because it will save time during play. You do not want to hold up the game, to the possible annoyance of the other players, whilst you try to make out the identity of a tile. Again, familiarity with the tiles will stop you making silly mistakes. The tiles are, after all, relatively small and discards (which are face up on the table) are displayed at random, which means that they can point in any direction (and cannot be moved once placed). It is useful in particular to be able to identify each of the four winds at a glance and also the Chinese numbers at the top of the tiles of the character suit, as the Arabic numerals on the tiles (and in some sets there are none) are invariably small. Between regular players, play is fast (it is considered discourteous to play slowly) – another reason to gain familiarity with the tiles.

In mahjong each player plays for him or herself – there are no partnerships. A player may, however, tacitly assist another player.

Object of the game

The overall aim is to accumulate the most points. The more immediate aim is to be the first player in each hand to go mahjong or to woo (harmony), which is the same thing. (You will come across a number of alternative words and phrases that have crept into the game.) Going mahjong is roughly equivalent to going 'rummy' in the card game of that name. The advantage of going mahjong is that in settling accounts everyone has to pay you and you pay nobody.

A **mahjong hand** is any complete hand; that is, one that consists of four sets and a pair. Bonus tiles – the flowers and seasons – form no part of a mahjong hand. When a mahjong hand is completed, the player declares it and exposes his rack for the other players to scrutinize. If the other players are satisfied that it is a mahjong hand, play ends. It is important to note that the player going mahjong does not discard. In addition, certain special hands that do not meet the above criteria of four sets and a pair are the equivalent of mahjong.

Sets

There are three types of sets, the **Chow**, the **Pung** and the **Kong**. The first two are each composed of three tiles and the third of four tiles.

A **chow** (run) is any three tiles of the same suit in **sequence**. The proper Chinese name for the chow is ch'i (chow is a vulgar term associated with food!) but almost everyone in the West calls it chow. Examples of chows are illustrated:

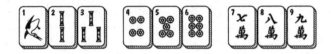

Notice that a chow is made up of precisely three tiles that cannot be extended. A chow may be concealed or exposed.

A **pung** is any three identical tiles. Examples of pungs are illustrated:

A pung may be concealed or exposed.

A **kong** is any four identical tiles. Examples of kongs are illustrated:

A kong may be concealed or exposed. A kong can be developed from a pung by adding the fourth tile.

A **pair** may be any two identical tiles. It has a number of names: the **sparrow's head**, the **eyes of the bird**, the **pillow**. A discard may not be claimed to complete a pair except if the discard allows the player to go mahjong. Notice that bonus tiles cannot form pairs as no two are identical. Below are examples of pairs.

A **concealed** set is one that was either complete in the original hand or has been completed by drawing from the wall. A concealed set does not contain discards.

An **exposed** set is one that includes a tile discarded by another player. The set is at once placed face up on the player's rack or on the table in front of the player. This action is called melding or grounding. An exposed set may only contain one discard.

Examples of mahjong hands

Sets may be concealed or exposed or a mixture of both in a mahjong hand. The pair is always concealed until the end of the game. A discard to complete a pair with a tile held in hand can only be claimed if it completes the mahjong hand.

A mahjong hand may number between 14 and 18 tiles, excluding bonus tiles, depending on the number of kongs it contains. These can range from none to four. Below are some examples of mahjong hands. Notice that despite the discrepancies in tile numbers, each hand contains the prescribed four sets and a pair:

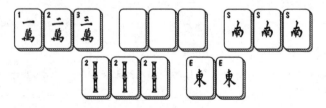

This hand contains 14 tiles. It has three pungs, a chow and a pair of winds. The sets may have been concealed or exposed or any combination of these.

This hand contains 15 tiles. It is composed of a kong, a pung, two chows and a pair of suit tiles.

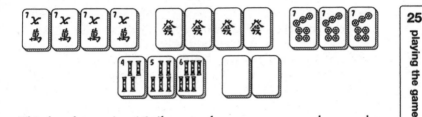

This hand contains 16 tiles; two kongs, a pung, a chow and a pair of white dragons.

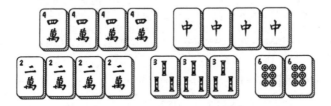

This hand has 17 tiles, three kongs, a pung and a pair of suit tiles.

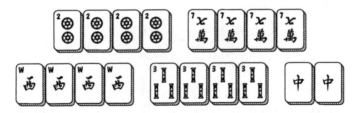

This highly unusual hand has 18 tiles, four kongs and a pair of red dragons.

Procedure

Declaration of bonus tiles

All players begin by declaring any bonus tiles they hold in their hands. Bonus tiles must be placed face up at the extreme right on the players' racks or on the table in front of them. Each player in turn, starting with East and moving anticlockwise, draws a replacement tile from the dead wall (kong box) for every bonus tile declared. (Millington requires replacements for bonus tiles to be drawn from the live wall, but this is immaterial.) If any further bonus tiles are drawn in this process, these must be declared in the same way and replacements drawn. There must always be a loose tile or tiles on the wall. When both loose tiles have been taken, the next stack is lifted and positioned as in the preliminary stage (the top tile is placed furthest from the start of the dead wall and is taken first).

If a player declares a bonus tile and omits to take a replacement, his hand will be a tile short and he will be unable to go mahjong. Any bonus tile drawn subsequently during play must at once be exposed and a replacement tile drawn in the same way. A bonus tile retained in the hand does not score and furthermore prevents the player from going mahjong because he is a tile short.

Declaration of kongs

Now East may declare any kongs held in his hand. He puts out the tiles on the table next to one another with either the two end or the two central tiles face up and the other two face down. This arrangement indicates that the set was concealed, necessary for scoring purposes (see diagram).

a concealed kong

East now takes a replacement tile from the kong box for each kong declared to keep his hand in balance. If a replacement tile is a bonus tile or completes another kong, then it too is declared and a replacement tile drawn, and so on. Although it is usual to declare a concealed kong at once it is not obligatory to do so and may be declared on any subsequent turn. The purpose in delaying the declaration would be to conceal the existence of the kong from the other players. However, a player will be unable to go mahjong without declaring it. The other three players, on their first or any subsequent turn, may in the same manner declare any kongs they hold.

Sequence of play

East is the prevailing wind of the first round. East, who drew an extra tile in the deal, now starts the game proper by discarding any tile from his hand. The tile is placed face up anywhere within the walls and at the same time East identifies it verbally, e.g. '8 of characters' as a courtesy to the other players. (Some experts prefer to play in silence, in which case the discarder taps the tile to indicate it to the other players.) Each player now has 13 tiles. It remains the responsibility of the other players to check the action of the turn player and to draw attention to any irregularities.

Heaven's Blessing, Earth's Blessing and Original Call

These three hands can occur only in the first round of play (i.e. on a player's first turn). It sometimes happens that East has the good fortune to pick up a complete mahjong hand. This is called, with good reason, **Heaven's Blessing**. East does not discard and exposes his hand for the other players to verify. When all are satisfied that it is a mahjong hand, the other players disclose their own hands. Scores are now calculated, settlement made, and the hand is at an end. If South, West or North go mahjong by claiming East's first discard or by drawing a winning tile from the wall on their first turn, it is known as **Earth's Blessing** and the same procedure is followed as with Heaven's Blessing.

If a player, after making his first discard, is one tile away from mahjong he may declare an **Original Call** or **Standing Hand**. He may not thereafter change his hand in any way other than by declaring bonus tiles. If he succeeds in going mahjong he scores an extra double (see scoring). These are predictably rare occurrences. Normally play continues until one player goes mahjong or the live wall is exhausted.

The turn

A player's normal turn consists of drawing a tile from the live wall or claiming the tile discarded by the previous player and is concluded by discarding a tile. The normal sequence of play after East's discard is South, West, North, then back to East. However, the sequence may be disrupted if a discard is claimed.

Drawing from the wall

In drawing tiles from the live wall, the top tile of the nearest stack must be taken. If only one tile remains in the stack, that must be taken.

Claiming a discard

Any player may claim the tile discarded by the previous player. However, a **discard** may be claimed only to complete a set or to go mahjong. There is a further restriction in that a discard to complete a chow may be claimed only by the player whose turn it is; that is, the player who is seated on the right of the discarder. This restriction does not apply if the tile is needed to complete a chow for mahjong. In the event of two or all three players claiming a discard there is a strict order of precedence. The player who requires the tile for mahjong has first claim, then the player who requires the tile for a pung and finally the player who wants the tile for a chow. The claim is made by announcing 'mahjong', 'pung' (or 'kong') or 'chow' as appropriate. In the unlikely event that more than one player claims a discard to go mahjong, the player next to play takes precedence. For example, East discards and both West and North call 'mahjong'. West wins the discard.

A discard may never be taken into hand. It can only be claimed to complete mahjong or a set, which must be melded face up (sometimes termed grounded) immediately. Once the next player has drawn a tile a discard is dead and remains dead for the rest of the game. It cannot be touched or moved at any time.

The sequence of play is disrupted if a player other than the player on the right of the discarder wins a discard. Supposing South discards and East claims a pung. East is obliged to expose the pung and then to discard to end the turn. The turn moves anti-clockwise so it is now South's turn again: West and North have in effect lost their turns. The diagram illustrates this sequence.

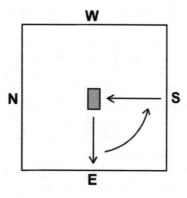

South discards, East claims discard and South plays again

Drawn game

A drawn game or wash-out occurs when the live wall is exhausted without any player having gone mahjong. The last 14 tiles of the wall, which include those remaining in the kong box, may not be used. When the kong box has been reduced, tiles may, if desired, be moved across from the far end of the live wall to keep the number of dead tiles to 14. This can be done at any convenient time during play.

A draw can also occur, although very rarely and then only by prior agreement, when three players all want the tile discarded by the fourth player for mahjong. When a wash-out occurs the hands are not scored and no settlements are made. The tiles are again placed face down and shuffled and the walls rebuilt. The dealer does not change.

Sets

Chows are the easiest sets to complete but they do not score, even if concealed. The advantage of chows is that they help you to complete a mahjong hand.

A pung, whether exposed or concealed, has the advantage of being capable of conversion into a kong. However, an exposed pung can be converted into a kong only with a tile drawn from the wall and never from a discard as it is a rule that no set may contain more than one discard.

A kong may be acquired in any of four ways:

1 A kong may be picked up in the original deal. This is a concealed kong.
2 A tile drawn from the wall may be added to an exposed pung to form an exposed kong.
3 A discard may be claimed and added to a concealed pung that is then melded (converted into an exposed kong).
4 A kong may be assembled entirely in hand. This is a concealed kong and corresponds to 1.

A player is not obliged to declare a concealed kong but cannot go mahjong unless and until he does. If in the meanwhile another player goes mahjong the kong counts only as a concealed pung. A concealed kong of honours is a high-scoring set.

Since one discard only is allowed in any set, a discard cannot be claimed to form a kong from an exposed pung.

Robbing the kong

If a player has an exposed pung and draws the fourth tile from the wall to complete a kong, a player who requires that tile for mahjong may appropriate it. This is called 'Robbing the kong'. The player who formed the kong does not draw a loose tile from the kong box and if he has done so before the kong has been robbed, he must return it. A concealed kong that has been melded can be robbed only to complete a **Thirteen Unique Wonders** hand (see Chapter 05 on Special Hands).

Calling

A player who needs one tile only to go out (mahjong) is said to be **calling**. A player does not announce this in the standard game.

Here is a calling hand:

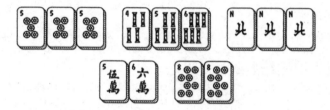

The hand is made up of three sets and a pair with an incomplete chow. The player is calling for either of two tiles, the 4 or 7 of characters. If the next tile from the wall was an 8 of circles, a concealed pung would yield an extra four points but then one of the character tiles would have to be discarded leaving a single tile to be matched for mahjong. Accordingly, the player might opt to forego the pung and discard the 8 of circles to keep the two chances for mahjong.

A player who needs to match a single tile in hand to go out is said to be **fishing**. A fishing hand is also a calling hand. A player does not announce this in the standard game. Here is an example of a fishing hand:

This hand is fishing for a 2 of circles. This would complete the required four sets and a pair for mahjong. Notice that no other tile will complete the hand. If, say, a west wind was discarded and claimed or the tile was drawn from the wall, this would complete a kong. Now a replacement tile would have to be drawn from the kong box. If it were another 2 of circles then the hand would be complete and mahjong would be called. In all probability, however, the player would find himself with two unlike tiles and would have to discard one of them when he would still be fishing.

Letting off a cannon

If a player announces that he is calling and has one or other of several powerful exposed hands, then another player who wilfully discards a tile consistent with that hand that allows the calling player to go mahjong is 'Letting off a cannon' and is severely punished (see Chapter 06 on Infringements and Penalties).

Significance of the winds

In each hand there is a **prevailing wind** and in addition each player has a personal wind that corresponds to his seat. The distinctions are for scoring purposes only.

The prevailing wind is the wind of the round (a minimum of four hands) and is predetermined. A player benefits if he has a pair of wind tiles that correspond to the prevailing wind, whether or not he goes mahjong. Note that this applies to all players.

A player benefits if he has a pair of wind tiles that correspond to his seat ('**own wind**'), whether or not he goes mahjong. Note that each player has a different wind so that, for instance, a pair of south wind tiles would be of value only to the player in the south seat if South were not the prevailing wind.

The seat wind of each player in rotation is also the prevailing wind.

A player scores twice if his pair of wind tiles is simultaneously the prevailing wind and his own wind, whether or not he goes mahjong.

The goulash

The **goulash**, common to some card games, may also be used in mahjong. The goulash follows the deal but before play begins. Properly it is only employed, if at all, after a wash-out. However, it is not a bad idea for inexperienced players to agree a goulash at the start of a game as it affords experience in evaluating a hand and then attempting to improve it. A goulash also tends to shorten the playing time, often dramatically, and so arguably makes the game more interesting, at least to the beginner. On the downside, it greatly increases the chance element and cannot be recommended for serious play. The goulash, by the way, has no connection with the old Chinese game. It is particularly associated with the modern American version (in which it is known, though in a slightly different form, as the **Charleston** or **Razzle**) and is sometimes adopted in other countries. Some players do not allow chows (except in special hands) when a goulash is played.

After the deal there is an exchange of tiles. Players examine their hands, select three tiles they do not want and place them face down in front of them. In the initial exchange, East and West exchange tiles, as do South and North. The players then examine their new hands and again select three tiles for exchange. The second exchange is between East and South and between West and North. The process is repeated for the third exchange, this time between East and North and between South and West. The exchanges may be made in a different order if preferred so long as each player exchanges once with every other player. Some players impose a minimum of two or even three doubles on a mahjong hand when a goulash has been played.

Here is a random deal prior to a goulash. The prevailing wind is South. East of course has been dealt an extra tile.

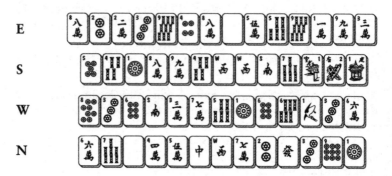

Now let us rearrange the hands as a help to deciding which tiles to pass:

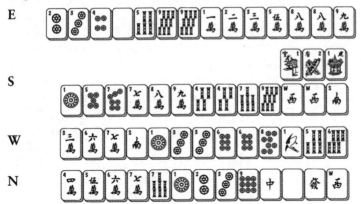

Consider East's hand. East will be anxious to go mahjong early because of the double points he will earn if he is the first to go out and the points penalty he will likely incur if he fails. However, he has a promising collection of character tiles and is tempted to discard the chow in circles (which of course is worth nothing) in the hope of inheriting more characters, even though this runs against his aim of an early mahjong. Eventually he decides to keep the circles and passes the 5 of bamboos, the white dragon and the 5 of characters to West.

South has a promising hand. He drew no fewer than three bonus tiles in the deal, one of them, the 2 of flowers, proper both to his seat and the wind of the round (prevailing wind). He then drew the 7 of characters, 7 of circles and 9 of bamboos as replacements for the bonus tiles, gaining a chow. He decides to discard the three circle tiles as he reasons (correctly) that he is slightly more likely to get an 8 of bamboos than a 6 of circles from an East discard. He passes the three circle tiles across to North.

West has a simple task in deciding which tiles to pass. He settles on the obvious: the 3 of characters, south wind and the 1 of bamboos, all of them isolated tiles.

North on the other hand has a problem. He has two chows and four random honours. He is tempted to hang on to the dragons, at least at this pass, and decides on the 7 of bamboos (an obvious choice), the 9 of circles and west wind, which he passes to South. The wind tile is neither the seat nor the wind of the round so is fairly safe, or so he reasons.

Here is a check on the tiles passed in the first exchange:

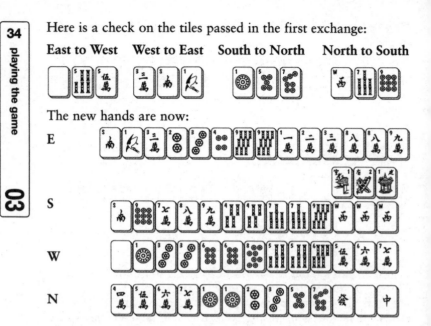

East to West   West to East   South to North   North to South

The new hands are now:

E

S

W

N

The second exchange is between East and South and between West and North. East is frustrated. None of the tiles he receives are the least help to him. He decides to pass them on. South on the other hand is delighted with the exchange: he now has a concealed pung of winds, worth 8 points. The 7 of bamboos creates another pair, only the 9 of circles is unhelpful.

South has two easy discards: the 9 of circles and the 9 of bamboos. A third tile is necessary and South reluctantly parts with his own wind.

West completes a chow as a result of the exchange and now has a pair of 5 of bamboos. The white dragon is useless. He decides to pass it on together with the 1 and 8 of circles.

North now has two chows but very little else. The extra character tile is superfluous so North decides to pass on the 4 and picks two of the dragons for surrender at random, the red and the green. This is a reluctant decision because they may well benefit West but it seems the only option. Here is a check on the tiles passed in the second exchange:

East to South	South to East	West to North	North to West

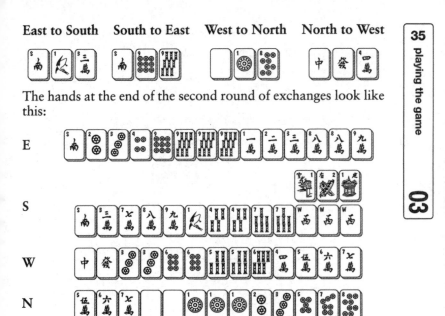

The hands at the end of the second round of exchanges look like this:

E

S

W

N

The exchange was one of mixed fortunes. East struck lucky this time completing a pung of terminals (9 of bamboos) and is getting close to mahjong. His chance of completing a pung of 8 of characters is almost as good (or as bad!) as compiling a chow. But he needs a pair anyway so the 9 of characters, 9 of circles and south wind are scheduled for disposal.

South has gained nothing from the exchange and passes on the same tiles that West fed to East and East passed on.

West also has gained nothing from the exchange. He has just one chow so his prospects of mahjong are dim. His game plan should be to go on the defensive; that is, playing to stop the other players scoring in preference to building his own hand. He passes the 4 of characters and the red and green dragons.

North has benefited handsomely. He now has a pung of terminals (1 of circles) and a pair of dragons — a very useful gain of 10 points. The third tile that he receives (8 of circles) will also do very well. Now any of the circle tiles 1, 4, 6 or 9 would yield a chow. North would therefore like to maintain the status quo but alas cannot do so. He has two options: to part with the 2, 3 and 5 of circles or the 5, 7 and 8. He elects for the former. Here is a check on the tiles passed in the third exchange:

| East to North | North to East | South to West | West to South |

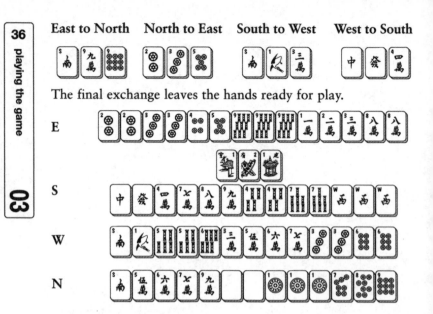

The final exchange leaves the hands ready for play.

East and North have shown gains. East has now a nice cluster of circle tiles. His first discard is likely to be the 5 of circles (remember, East is anxious to go mahjong quickly). Now he will be calling for a 1 or 4 of circles to go mahjong. South's hand qualifies for a useful score but he is a long way from going out. West's hand is miserable. It does not score at all. All that can be said for it is that it has three pairs, which offer chances for pungs. North on the other hand has done very well. His initial hand was worthless but now it is not only worth 10 points but it is one tile away from fishing. This illustrates well the chance factor of the goulash.

Etiquette

Etiquette in mahjong is partly a matter of convention and partly a matter of courtesy and common sense.

1 A tile turned over during washing must be thoroughly mixed.
2 If you have completed building your section of the wall help others to complete theirs.
3 Do not look at your tiles during the deal. Wait until all have been dealt.
4 If a player exposes a tile he would have drawn he must take it.

5 Do not discuss the game at any time.
6 Do not reveal information on your hand to the other players, whether in good faith or with intent to deceive.
7 No player may ask for information about another player's hand.
8 Play fast. Amongst experienced players, slow play is a major crime!

04 scoring and settlement

In this chapter you will learn:
- how hands are scored
- how accounts are settled
- scoring variations.

The **points** awarded for sets and hands in mahjong are traditional and largely arbitrary; they do not reflect, in many cases, the relative difficulty in achieving them.

Scoring and **settlement** are the responsibility of all the players except in the event of a wash-out when the hand is cancelled and no-one scores. When play is at an end, each player adds up the value of their own hands. This is usually done in rotation, starting with East and proceeding anticlockwise round the table. Each player's score is monitored in turn by the others. Scores are recorded in points. Mistakes are not uncommon, even amongst experienced players, underlining the need for careful checking. Phenomenal totals are theoretically possible, making it necessary to impose a limit. Scoring is in two stages, first a basic score for a hand is established. The hand may then be entitled to one or more doubles which, when applied, give a final score. When all hands are scored players settle accounts with each other.

- Doubles: A hand may be entitled to one or more doubles of the basic score. A double simply doubles the basic score, two doubles double the basic score twice, and so on. Some doubles apply only to the player who goes mahjong, others apply to all players.
- The Limit: A maximum score on any one hand, called a limit, is set before the game. The limit is commonly 500 or 1000 points but any limit (or no limit) can be agreed between the players. This means that a player who achieves a score above the limit is considered to have scored the limit, any excess being disregarded.
- Special and limit hands: Certain rare hands are not scored because they are defined as limit hands and automatically qualify for maximum payment. In addition, some players award points for limit hands that are calling. These are all covered in the next chapter.

The basic score

The basic **score** of a hand is the sum of points awarded to bonus tiles and to sets and pairs in the hand, whether concealed or exposed. Notice that chows do not score, whether concealed or exposed and that concealed sets of pungs and kongs score double the points of the same sets exposed. Below are the scores awarded to a basic hand. Pairs are, by definition, concealed.

Exposed sets		*Pairs*	
Chow:	0 pts	Pair of dragons:	2 pts
Pung of minor tiles:	2 pts	Pair of own wind:	2 pts
Pung of major tiles:	4 pts	Pair of prevailing wind:	2 pts
Kong of minor tiles:	8 pts	Pair of own wind	
Kong of major tiles:	16 pts	if also prevailing wind:	4 pts
		– other pairs do not score.	

Concealed sets

Chow:	0 pts
Pung of minor tiles:	4 pts
Pung of major tiles:	8 pts
Kong of minor tiles:	16 pts
Kong of major tiles:	32 pts

Explanation *'Own wind' and 'prevailing wind' mean wind tiles corresponding to the player's seat and the wind of the round (prevailing wind) respectively.*

Bonus Tiles

Flowers, each:	4 pts
Seasons, each:	4 pts

Player going mahjong

The player who goes mahjong has opportunities for scoring not available to the other players. The following points can be scored only by the player going out:

For going mahjong:	10 pts
Mahjong with only possible tile:	2 pts

Explanation *Mahjong with the only possible tile means that one value only is required for mahjong. For example, the middle value of a chow, or the value needed to complete a chow that includes a terminal, or a matching tile to complete a pair. Going mahjong with the only possible tile is also known as 'filling the only place'. Examples: if a player holds the 6 and 8 or the 8 and 9 of a suit, a 7 in the same suit, provided it completes a mahjong hand, would earn 2 points; however, if instead the player holds a 7 and 8 of the same suit this would not qualify since the chow could be completed with either a 6 or a 9. If two or more different tiles will allow a player to go mahjong but all except one have already been played (melded and/or discarded), then this value becomes the only possible tile and scores accordingly.*

Final tile drawn from the wall: 2 pts

Explanation The last tile to complete the hand is drawn from the wall; that is, it is not a discard by another player. If this happens to be the only possible tile ('filling the only place', above) then 4 points are scored.

Winning by fishing the eyes: 2 pts or 4 pts

Explanation If a player has four sets and a single tile and matches the tile (to complete a pair) to go mahjong either by drawing from the wall or claiming a discard, he scores 2 points if the tiles are simples and 4 points if they are majors. A player who fishes the last tile may score an additional 2 points for drawing the tile from the wall.

Doubles

The following doubles are scored only by the player going mahjong:

One double
Winning from the bottom of the sea
Explanation Player goes mahjong with the last tile from the live wall, i.e., the 15th tile from the end, leaving the 14 'dead' tiles (including those remaining in the kong box) on the table.

Catching a fish from the bottom of the river
Explanation Player goes mahjong with the last tile from the live wall which has been drawn and discarded.

Winning on the roof
Explanation Completing the hand by drawing a loose tile from the dead wall.

Opening a flower
Explanation If the last tile of the live wall completes a kong or is a bonus tile, or if the last tile is discarded and claimed for a kong, and in either case the player draws a replacement tile from the dead wall (thus reducing the remaining tiles to 13) and goes mahjong with it, this is called 'Opening a Flower'. Notice that this hand would also qualify for a double for 'Winning on the roof'.

One double is awarded for any of the following hands. These are explained below:

Hand of all chows and a non-scoring pair
Hand without chows

Hand of honour tiles and one suit only
Hand of major tiles with any pair
Robbing the kong

Hand of all chows and a non-scoring pair
Explanation This is a non-scoring hand but points for bonus tiles, final tile from wall, fishing, etc., are not excluded.

Hand without chows
Explanation This hand is known as 'Birds singing in harmony'.

Hand of honour tiles and one suit only
Explanation This hand is unrestricted as to sets but must not include more than one suit together with winds and/or dragons.

Hand of major tiles and any pair
Explanation A hand composed of sets of major tiles (honours or terminals) with any pair. By definition, the hand contains no chows.

Robbing the kong
Explanation This was explained in Chapter 03.

The above hands qualify without distinction as to whether sets are concealed or exposed. Doubles are cumulative. For example, in a hand of major tiles with any pair (one double) the hand might contain a set of red dragons and a set of own wind, which would earn two further doubles making three doubles of the basic score for the hand.

Two doubles
Hand (including the pair) of major tiles only.

Three doubles
Hand (including the pair) composed of a single suit only (no honour tiles).

Limit hands
Certain unique ways of going mahjong score the limit. These are explained in the next chapter.

All players
The following doubles are scored by all players, whether or not the player in question goes mahjong and whether or not the sets are concealed or exposed.

One double
Pung or kong of dragons
Pung or kong of prevailing wind
Pung or kong of own wind
All four flower tiles (bouquet)
All four season tiles (bouquet)
Player's flower and season (pair)
Three concealed pungs
Two sets of dragons and pair of third dragon
Three sets of winds and pair of fourth wind

Some of these are explained below.

Bonus tiles
Explanation A player's flower or season is dictated by the seat he is occupying; thus: East = 1, South = 2, West = 3, North = 4.

Three concealed pungs
Explanation A double is awarded for a hand containing three concealed pungs, which may include any concealed pung for which a discard has been claimed to complete a kong.

Two sets of dragons and pair of third dragon

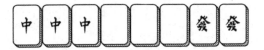

Known as the Three Lesser (or Little) Scholars. Note that this hand is incomplete. Two further sets are needed for mahjong.

Explanation This double is in addition to the two doubles earned for the two sets of dragons, giving a total of three doubles on the basic hand.

Three sets of winds and pair of fourth wind

Known as the Four Little Joys or the Four Lesser (or Little) Blessings. Note that this hand is incomplete. A further set is needed for mahjong.

Explanation This double is in addition to double(s) earned for own and/or prevailing wind.

Two doubles
Three sets of dragons

Known as the Three Great Scholars or the Big Three Dragons.

Explanation These doubles are in addition to doubles already earned; thus the Three Great Scholars would earn a double for each set of dragons. Added to the two doubles for completing the three sets gives a total of five doubles for the hand. Notice that this is not a mahjong hand as it requires an additional pung and a pair. If the hand was complete it would earn a limit (see next chapter).

Four sets of winds

Known as the Four Large Blessings or the Big Four Joys.

Explanation These two doubles are in addition to doubles already earned; thus Four Large Blessings would earn a double for a set of the prevailing wind, another double for a set of the player's own wind and a third double for an 'all major tiles' hand. Added to the two doubles for 'Four Large Blessings' gives a total of five doubles on the basic score. Notice that this is not a mahjong hand as it omits the pair. If a pair were added to the above this would rank as a limit hand (see next chapter).

Doubling
A player's basic score is multiplied the number of times indicated by the number of doubles earned:

One double	– multiply basic score by 2
Two doubles	– ,, ,, ,, by 4
Three doubles	– ,, ,, ,, by 8
Four doubles	– ,, ,, ,, by 16
Five doubles	– ,, ,, ,, by 32

Six doubles   – multiply basic score by 64
Seven doubles –   ,,   ,,   ,,   by 128
Eight doubles   –   ,,   ,,   ,,   by 256
. . . and so on.

Scoring a hand

Scoring needs practice. Six sample hands are scored below. Follow these through as an aid to familiarization.

①

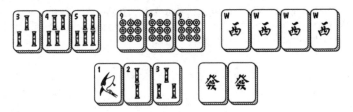

Situation West goes mahjong with the above hand. The prevailing wind was East. The pung of 9 of circles was concealed; the other sets were exposed. There are no bonus tiles. West scores the basic hand as follows:

For going mahjong	10 pts
Pung of terminals (concealed)	8 pts
Kong of winds (exposed)	16 pts
Pair of dragons	2 pts
Total:	36 pts

Doubles One double for a kong of own wind = 36 points × 2. Thus the score for the hand is 72 points. West will receive 144 points from East and 72 points from each of the other players.

②

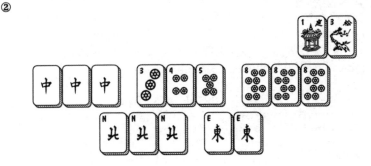

Situation East goes mahjong with the above hand. The prevailing wind was South. The tiles were exposed apart from the pung of dragons and of course the pair. East scores:

For going mahjong	10 pts
Two bonus tiles	8 pts
Pung of dragons (concealed)	8 pts
Pung of simples (exposed)	2 pts
Pung of winds (exposed)	4 pts
Pair of own wind	2 pts
Total:	34 pts

Doubles One double for hand of honour tiles and one suit only. Another double for a pung of dragons, thus $34 \times 2 \times 2 = 136$. East receives double so East will get 272 points from each of the other players.

③

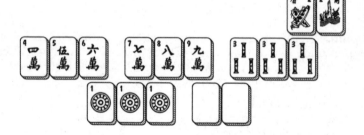

Situation South goes mahjong with the above hand. The prevailing wind was North. The hand was concealed apart from the pung of terminals and South drew the last tile from the wall. South scores:

For going mahjong	10 pts
Two bonus tiles	8 pts
Pung of simples	4 pts
Pung of terminals (exposed)	4 pts
Pair of dragons	2 pts
Final tile from wall	2 pts
Total:	30 pts

Doubles One double for the player's flower and season $2 \times 30 = 60$ points. South will receive 120 points from East and 60 points from each of the other players.

④

Situation North goes mahjong with the above hand. The prevailing wind was West. The pung was exposed but the rest of the hand was concealed. North scores:

For going mahjong:	10 pts
Pung of simples (exposed)	2 pts
<u>Total:</u>	12 pts

Doubles None. North will receive 24 points from East and 12 points from the other players.

⑤

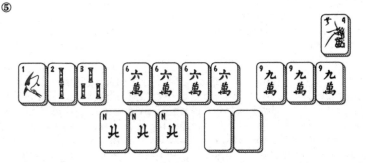

Situation South goes mahjong with the above hand. The prevailing wind was North. The kong and the pung of winds were exposed, the hand having been completed by robbing East of the 3 of bamboos. South scores:

For going mahjong	10 pts
Bonus tile	4 pts
Kong of simples (exposed)	8 pts
Pung of terminals (concealed)	8 pts
Pung of winds (exposed)	4 pts
Pair dragons	2 pts
<u>Total:</u>	36 pts

Doubles One double for robbing the kong. Hence total score 36 × 2 = 72 points. South receives 144 points from East and 72 points from each of the other players.

⑥

Situation East goes mahjong with the above very big hand. The whole hand was concealed. The prevailing wind was East. East scores:

For going mahjong	10 pts
Five bonus tiles	20 pts
Pung of winds (concealed)	8 pts
Pung of dragons (concealed)	8 pts
Kong of dragons (concealed)	32 pts
Kong of terminals (concealed)	32 pts
Pair of dragons	2 pts
<u>Total:</u>	112 pts

Doubles One double for hand of honour tiles and one suit only; another double for hand of no chows, a double for a bouquet of season tiles, a double for a pung of own wind, a double for a pung of prevailing wind, a double for the Three Lesser Scholars and finally two doubles for a hand of major tiles including the pair, a total of eight doubles of the basic hand. This gives 112 × 256 = 28,672. This massive total qualifies as a limit hand so all players pay East 2000 points (1000 doubled for East wind).

Even this hand pales when measured against the largest hand possible, which someone somewhere may have held at some time. The player who is North completes the final kong by drawing the last tile from the wall then drawing the south wind from the kong box to complete the hand. South is the prevailing wind and all sets are concealed.

The hand show below, which includes 22 doubles, is worth over 46 million points. If it ever occurred, the other players must have been grateful for the limit!

Settlement

The winner is defined as the player who went mahjong. The three losers pay the winner the point count, including doubles, if any, of his hand. If East wins the other players pay him double. The losers then settle amongst themselves paying or receiving the difference in their scores with East paying or receiving double. By way of illustration, here are the tiles held by the four players at the end of a hand.

Situation West goes mahjong; the prevailing wind is South.

West's hand is exposed except for the chow of circles and the pair of dragons. West scores 10 points (mahjong), 8 points (bonus tiles), kong of bamboos 8 points, pung of bamboos 2 points, pair of dragons 2 points, no doubles, total 30 points.

N

North's hand is exposed apart from the odd tiles. North scores 4 points for the bonus tile, 4 points for the pung of winds and 2 points for the pung of simples. He earns one double for the pung of the prevailing wind, a total of 20 points.

E

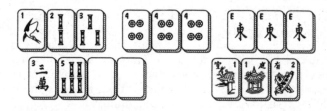

East's hand is concealed apart from the odd tiles. East scores 12 points for the bonus tiles, 4 points for the pung of simples and 8 points for the pung of winds, total 24 points. He earns a double for player's flower and season and another double for pung of own wind, plus 2 points for a pair of dragons, a total of 98 points.

S

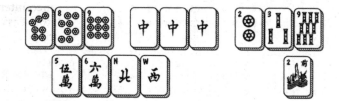

South's hand is concealed except for the pung of dragons. South scores 4 points for the bonus tile and 4 points for the pung of dragons. He earns one double for the pung of dragons making a total of 16 points.

West receives 60 points (i.e. double) from East, 30 points from North and 30 points from South. West is therefore up 120 points on the hand.

East has 98 points against North's 20 points, a difference of 78, but East is entitled to double so gains 156 points. He also has an advantage of 82 points against South and again scores double, 164 points. East therefore profits by 260 points (156 + 164 − 60) on the hand.

North has 20 points against South's 16 points so gains 4 points but has to pay 30 points to West and 156 points to East. North is down 182 points.

South loses 4 points to North, 30 points to West and 164 points to East so is down 198 points on the hand.

Comment
Although West went mahjong, East is by far the biggest winner on the hand with South and North both losing heavily. The hand demonstrates the importance of East's position; he can be a big winner (as here) but also a big loser. It also demonstrates the impact of doubles. The total of plus scores and the total of minus scores on a hand must of course always tally.

Scoring variations

One of the commonest scoring variations is to award 20 points rather than 10 points for mahjong. Clearly the doubled points make mahjong an attractive option when the alternative is to attempt to increase the value of the hand at the risk of another player going out first.

Other variations vary from the sensible to the idiosyncratic. Given here are those that are most commonly encountered. Perhaps the most important aspect of these, all too easy to overlook, is that any variation from the scoring system described above is likely to have impact on the play.

Some players allow one double for own flower and another double for own season. This increases the chance factor and is not recommended. On the other hand, adding any scores for bonus tiles after the hand has been valued (i.e. after any doubles have been executed) reduces their impact and hence the chance element in the game.

There are two innovations that can add appreciably to a player's score, an award for a standing (or calling) hand and an award for the player who is calling for a limit hand but fails to make it.

Standing hand
If East, after his first discard, is left with a calling hand (one tile required for mahjong) he can declare a 'standing hand'. Hereon he may not change his hand and is obliged to discard any tile

drawn from the wall if he cannot go mahjong. The tile to complete the hand may be a discard or drawn from the wall. Any other player may call a standing hand after their first discard whether on their turn they claimed a discard or took a tile from the wall. The reward for the player who completes a standing hand is 100 points in addition to his basic score.

Calling a limit

A player calling for a special (limit) hand (see next chapter) who fails to go out is commonly awarded 40% of the limit; thus 400 points if the limit is 1000 points. Similarly, a player who is calling a half-limit receives 200 points if he fails to achieve the hand. The player may announce that he is calling or he may not, as previously agreed. This award encourages players to try for special hands.

special hands

In this chapter you will learn:
- situations that earn maximum points
- 18 special hands
- 12 optional special hands.

In mahjong there are a number of special hands (also called limit hands) that earn big rewards because they are rare and difficult to achieve. Most players are lucky if they see more than one or two of these hands in a lifetime. The admissibility or otherwise of individual hands is probably the major cause of confusion and disagreement between players so it is strongly recommended that valid hands are agreed before play. These special hands can be divided into two groups; those that are completed in a unique manner regardless of content and those that are composed of nominated sets or individual tiles that form logical and easily recognized combinations. Hands in the first group are for the most part pure chance; in contrast, those in the second group are deliberately collected. The proliferation of hands in this second group (fancy hands are all too easy to invent) has been a negative factor in the development of the game and this has not been helped by the confusing number of names given to them. The early Chinese game recognized a few special hands but the temptation in the West to introduce more and more limit hands with romantic names has proved compelling. Instead of a dozen to a score of original special hands, today you could be faced with close on 100 depending on what version of mahjong you are playing and who you are playing with.

A special hand of the second group is extremely difficult to complete, particularly in the old Chinese game as expounded here. This is because mahjong hands are not difficult to assemble provided that a player is content with a modest reward. If you are alert to the danger of a special hand being formed by another player, you will be wise to take the quickest route to mahjong, which probably means going for chows at the expense of scoring sets.

Special hands are a little easier to achieve if one or other of the modern restrictions is placed on the composition of mahjong hands such as cleared (one suit only) hands and one-double hands (minimum of one double in hand before going mahjong — see Chapter 10 on American mahjong). Another variant that offers some encouragement to players contemplating special hands is the one-chow limitation recommended by Robertson.

Whatever restrictions, if any, are in force, a special hand in the second group, with one or two exceptions, should not be attempted unless most of the tiles needed are present in the original hand. Those hands that can claim a classical history (i.e., the original Chinese limit hands) are recommended, whilst those lacking a pedigree are best omitted. Whatever decision you reach, the inescapable fact is that all the players will need to be familiar with the limit hands in force. An idea is to have agreed hands listed on a sheet of paper that is available for reference during play.

Listed below are the six hands in the first group. All are 'special situations' and all except 7, which must be a very rare occurrence indeed, are matters of pure chance beyond the control of the player. The hands however add a certain charm to the game if only by the resonance of their names, although the chance of actually encountering any of them in play is remote.

1 **Catching the Moon from the Bottom of the Sea.** If the last tile of the live wall is the 1 of circles and a player goes mahjong with this he earns the limit.
2 **Heaven's Blessing.** East scores a limit if the hand dealt is a mahjong hand. Also known as the 'natural winning' or 'original call'.
3 **Earth's Blessing.** South, West or North go out with East's first discard. This also earns the limit.
4 **Kong on Kong.** If a player, in drawing a replacement tile for a kong, completes another kong the replacement tile for which allows the player to go mahjong (bonus tiles disregarded), this earns the limit.
5 **Scratching a carrying pole.** If a player goes out by robbing a kong of the 2 of bamboos it is a limit hand.
6 **Gathering plum blossom from the roof.** If a player goes out by drawing a 5 of circles from the kong box it is a limit hand.
7 *Thirteenth consecutive mahjong.* If East goes mahjong for the 13th consecutive time, wash-outs disregarded, he scores the limit. Also known as **'Lucky Thirteen'.** (An alternative and more realistic award, also confined to East, allows a half-limit for the sixth consecutive mahjong and a limit for the seventh and subsequent mahjongs.)

Merits of special hands

A **limit hand** is just what it says; it earns the maximum number of points previously agreed. But the hands are by no means equal. All hands of the second group can be subdivided into two categories: those that are valueless unless achieved, and those that can earn points regardless of whether they are completed or not. The first category has another disadvantage: all tiles except the last must be drawn from the wall. A hand in the first category should not normally be attempted unless at the very least two-thirds of the tiles are obtained in the deal. Discards should be judicious: a pung drawn from the wall will offer a crumb of comfort in the event of failure.

A hand of the second category, with its potential for scoring points even though it fails to be completed, has another advantage: it is often easy to switch into a mahjong hand if fortune disappoints. Because of these advantages, a special hand in this category can be attempted with a less favourable draw. In the following hands, 'concealed' means that no discards may be claimed except the last tile of the hand, whilst 'exposed' means that any discards may be claimed to make sets in the normal way – but remember that exposed sets may reveal your intentions. When attempting limit hands be careful not to assemble your tiles in such a way as to reveal your intentions.

First category

Heavenly Twins

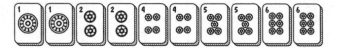

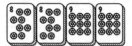

Seven pairs of tiles, all of one suit. This is a difficult hand to attain if only because it must be collected from the wall apart from the last tile, which can be a discard. It will probably be evident to the other players that you are collecting circles (you are discarding the other two suits) so that it is unlikely that any player will complete your hand for you. In this and the following two hands a kong (which is not declared as all three hands are concealed) can count as two pairs. If another player goes mahjong the kong will only score as a concealed pung. Concealed: a limit.

All Pairs

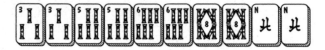

Seven pairs, all of one suit, but also winds and dragons in any mix. The same stricture applies as to the previous hand: collecting a single suit soon becomes evident to the other players. Easier to obtain than the Heavenly Twins. Concealed: a half-limit.

All Pair Honours

Pairs of dragons, winds or terminals. Not strictly an honours hand as the terminals are major, not honour tiles. If prospects appear poor for the hand, there is a good chance of converting one or two pairs into high-scoring pungs. Concealed: a limit.

Gertie's Garter

The 1–7 of one suit and 1–7 of another suit (sequences 2–8 and 3–9 are knitting hands). Concealed: a limit.

Knitting

Pairs made up of the same values of any two suits. Pairs cannot be repeated: they must all be of different values. Concealed: a half-limit.

Triple Knitting

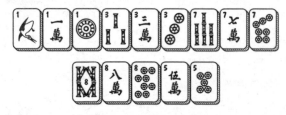

Triplets made up of the same values of each of the three suits and a random pair from different suits. A hand to be abandoned early if prospects do not improve rapidly. Concealed: a half-limit.

Thirteen Unique Wonders

Also known as the **Thirteen Grades of Imperial Treasure** and the **Thirteen Marvellous Lanterns**. The 1 and 9 of each suit, one each of winds and dragons, any tile paired. This hand has the advantage that the player's discards will reveal little. The hand is destroyed by anyone holding a kong in major tiles. Concealed: a limit.

Wriggly Snake

The 1–9 of one suit, one of every wind, one tile paired. Another single-suit hand that has to be acquired in the deal or drawn from the wall so discards are likely to arouse suspicions. Concealed: a limit.

Another version of this hand calls for a set of 1s and a set of 9s, a pair of 2s, 5s or 8s (the snake's eyes) and two chows made up of the six missing values, all tiles of the same suit. Exposed: a limit.

Windy Chow

One chow in each suit; one of each wind with one wind paired; this is one of the easiest hands to complete. Concealed (chows cannot be claimed): a half-limit.

Second category

Imperial Jade

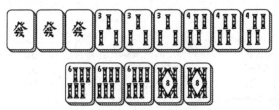

Hand made up entirely of green tiles. These are the 2s, 3s, 4s, 6s and 8s of bamboos and the green dragons (optional). The four sets may include one chow (2, 3, 4) if desired. Exposed: a limit.

All Honours

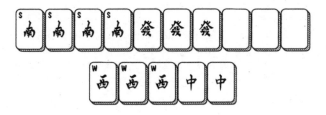

Hand composed of all honour tiles (four sets and a pair). Exposed: a limit.

Fourfold Plenty

Also known as the **Four Large Blessings**. Four kongs with any pair. A high-scoring hand even if mahjong is not achieved. Exposed: a limit.

Buried Treasure

Four sets in one suit with or without honour tiles and any pair. Concealed: a limit. An alternative hand calls for any four pungs and a pair with the last tile drawn from the wall. Concealed: a limit.

Gates of Heaven

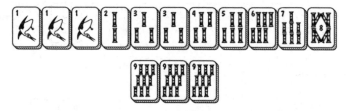

Also called **Heavenly Gates, Nine Gates** and **Nine United Sons**. The hand is calling with two sets of terminals and a run of simples 2–8, all in the same suit. This is a unique hand, as any tile 1–9 would then give mahjong (a 3 of bamboos in the example given). This hand is discussed in detail in a later chapter. Concealed: a limit.

Heads and Tails

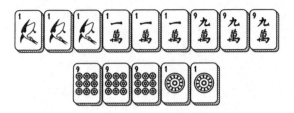

Four sets of terminals (any suit) together with a pair of terminals. A rewarding hand since it will score highly even if it does not succeed. Exposed: a limit.

Purity

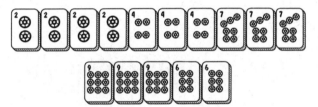

Any four pungs/kongs and a pair, all in the same suit. A difficult hand to achieve. Exposed: a limit.

Four Large Blessings

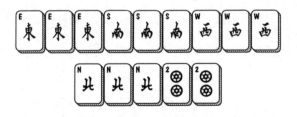

Also called **Four Joys in Full** or **Big Four Joys**. A set (pung or kong) of each of the winds with any pair. Again, a once-in-a-lifetime achievement with the comfort that each set scores. Exposed: a limit.

Three Great Scholars

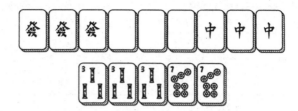

Also called the **Big Three Dragons**. A set of each of the dragons plus any pung or kong and a pair. Exposed: a limit.

The above special hands are practically universal and are an adequate repertoire for the average player. If special hands appeal to you, however, those below may be ranked as 'second division'. Even after absorbing these you will still be aware of only a fraction of the fancy hands that have been published world-wide.

Royal Ruby

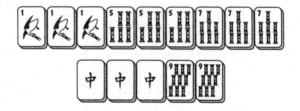

A ruby hand is composed of pungs or kongs of any of 1s, 5s, 7s and 9s of bamboos and red dragons. The hand is drawn from very few values and merits a double limit. Notice that this is a harder hand than Imperial Jade above because there is one value less to choose from. Exposed: a limit.

Ruby Jade

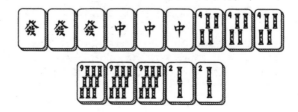

A hand composed of four pungs and a pair. The pungs must include a set of red dragons, a set of green dragons, a set of red bamboos and a set of green bamboos with any bamboo pair. Exposed: a limit.

Ruby Hand

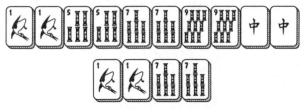

Seven pairs of red tiles (red bamboos/red dragons). Since there are only five qualifying tiles, two kongs (undeclared) divided into two pairs each will be necessary for this hand. Concealed: a limit.

Greta's Garden

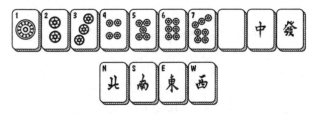

The 1–7 of any suit; one each of winds and dragons. Concealed: a limit.

Windfall

Five pairs of any one suit plus one each of the winds. Concealed: a limit.

Dragon's Breath

Five pairs of any one suit, one of each dragon plus one paired. Concealed: a limit.

Dragon's Tail

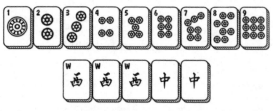

The 1–9 of one suit, plus either a pung of winds and a pair of dragons or a pung of dragons and a pair of winds. Concealed: a limit.

Dragonet

Three pairs of one suit plus a pair of honours and six odd honours. Concealed: a limit.

Five Odd Honours

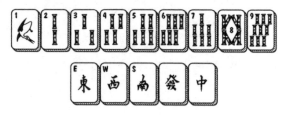

The 1–9 in a suit plus five odd honours. Concealed: a limit.

Dragonfly

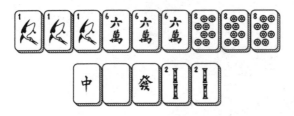

Three pungs, one in each suit plus one of each dragon and any two suit tiles paired. Concealed: a limit. Exposed: a half-limit.

Dirty Pairs

Seven pairs of anything. Concealed: a half-limit.

Clean Pairs

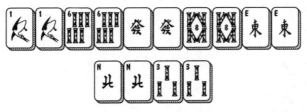

Pairs of honours and pairs of one suit only. Concealed: a limit.

infringements and penalties

In this chapter you will learn:
- mistakes that are not penalized
- infringements that carry a penalty
- why not to 'let off a cannon'.

Infringements of the rules usually incur **penalties**. In social games, penalties can be ignored but it is good discipline (and practice) to enforce them, or at least the most serious of them. If you are therefore playing mahjong socially it would be as well to agree beforehand which penalties, if any, are to be enforced. There is no authority for penalties but those given below are generally accepted. Those involving obscure infringements, not given here, should be agreed between the players. As a good general rule, a play once made (e.g. a discard, tile drawn from wall) cannot be retracted.

Inaccuracies

The following situations incur no penalty:

1 Player calls discard incorrectly.
2 Incorrect tile drawn from wall. Player must replace it. If it is exposed, all players must see the tile prior to replacement. Six stacks of tiles including the exposed tile are shuffled and rebuilt.
3 Player miscalls set but corrects it before discarding.
4 Player incorrectly calls mahjong but corrects this before any other player has disclosed their hand.
5 If a tile is accidentally dislodged from the wall and is seen by any player proceed as in 2.
6 If a player omits to take a replacement tile for a kong or bonus tile, he may do so on any subsequent turn provided no other player has declared a kong or bonus tile respectively in the meantime, otherwise the hand is dead.

Letting off a cannon

This is not strictly a rule infringement but it nevertheless incurs a harsh penalty. If a player announces that he is calling and his hand is made up of any of the following exposed sets and subsequently another player discards a tile which allows the first player to complete the hand, he has 'let off a cannon' (committed a howling blunder). Note that these are all potentially high-scoring hands.

1 If two sets of dragons are exposed a player may not discard a tile of the third dragon.
2 If three sets of winds are exposed a player may not discard a tile of the fourth wind.

3 If three sets of terminals are exposed a player may not discard a terminal.
4 If three sets of a single suit are exposed a player may not discard a tile of that suit.
5 If three sets of green tiles (bamboos/dragons) are exposed a player may not discard a green bamboo or dragon.
6 If three sets of honour tiles (dragons/winds) are exposed a player may not discard an honour tile.

Penalty

If a player lets off a cannon by committing any of the above offences he pays the winner as well as the debts of the other two players, a just punishment. In this event, the other two losing players do not settle between themselves. However, if the offending player has a waiting hand or no tiles in hand except forbidden tiles, he incurs no penalty.

Infringements

Infringement

A player who has too many or too few tiles has a **dead**, or **impure** hand.

Penalty

A player whose hand has been declared dead cannot go mahjong but may continue to play in the hope of a wash-out.

If the hand is long, a player may not score his hand and must pay all other players. A gentler punishment is for the left-hand player, on the offender's turn, to take a tile at random from the player's concealed hand and place it face up on the table. This is the player's discard. He does not draw.

If the hand is short, he may score his hand in the usual way, although some players disallow a short hand to claim doubles. The offender may never complete a set, either from the wall or from the table, if it leaves him without a discard.

Infringement

Player discloses a hand that contains any undisclosed bonus tiles but is otherwise correct.

Penalty

Player cannot go out and the bonus tiles do not score.

Infringement

Incorrect declaration of mahjong when at least one other player
has exposed their hand or part of it.

Penalty

Player must pay the half-limit to the other players.

Infringement

Incorrect set is declared and play continues when error is
discovered.

Penalty

The player's hand is dead.

Infringement

Player draws from the wall before or after the previous player
has discarded and claims the discard.

Penalty

Player may not claim discard. If another player claims discard,
the tile drawn must be replaced on the wall. If the tile was seen,
it must be shown to all players then shuffled with the nearest six
stacks of tiles before replacement.

Infringement

Player names his discard but retracts before releasing it.

Penalty

If another player claims the discard, then it must be played. If
the tile was falsely called and the player has a called tile in hand,
it must be discarded, even if it means breaking a set.

Infringement

Player puts down an incorrect set (chow, pung, kong).

Penalty

The set stays exposed but the player cannot go mahjong.

Infringement

Player claims a discard but cannot meld.

Penalty

If it is still the player's turn, he may put back the discard without penalty and take back into his hand any tiles that he has attempted to meld. If the discrepancy is discovered later, the set stands, the player is unable to go mahjong and must pay 100 points to the winner.

Infringement

A player fails to declare a bonus tile before making a discard.

Penalty

The offender must play with a short hand and therefore cannot go mahjong.

elementary strategy

In this chapter you will learn:
- to evaluate your hand
- the importance of discards
- hints on play.

Luck or skill?

First impressions are that mahjong is a game of chance. After all, you have no control over the deal, nor do you have any influence over the tiles you and your opponents draw from the wall, which by definition was assembled at random, and you have no say in the discards of the other players. This is an illusion but there is indeed a high chance element in the game, although this tends to cancel out in the way that multiple dice rolls even out. The skill element may not be immediately apparent but it is nevertheless a major factor in the game. Strong players win consistently, whatever their initial hands.

Mahjong is a game of imperfect information (in contrast to perfect information games like chess and backgammon). In the beginning you see only the tiles in your own hand plus any bonus tiles declared. As the game progresses, however, more and more information becomes available to you, although at no time during play do you have the complete picture. Information comes from two principal sources: discards and your opponents' melds (exposed sets). For the alert player there is additional intelligence in the behaviour of the other players; for example, tile arrangement, long thought, hesitation, body language. In older sets, discolouration and other imperfections can give clear signals to the unscrupulous (your opponents) who thereby gain an unfair advantage over more honest players like yourself.

Count your tiles!

It quite often happens during play that a player finds themselves with a tile short or an extra tile. It is good discipline to check constantly from the outset that you have the right number of tiles on your rack. If you have not, then you can never go mahjong and will be heavily penalized. The following are common causes of an imbalance.

Tile short

1 Failure to draw a replacement tile from the dead wall on melding a kong. Remember that if you have a concealed kong that you have not melded because you wish to deny the opponents the information, you will have to declare it and draw a replacement before you can go mahjong. You cannot draw a replacement tile and keep the kong concealed.
2 Failure to draw a replacement tile when declaring a bonus tile.

Excess tile

1 Failure to discard after claiming a tile from the table or drawing a tile from the wall.
2 After declaring a bonus tile, you draw a replacement and you then draw another tile from the live wall before discarding.

Evaluating your hand

An important element in the appraisal of your hand is tile distribution. To overlook this lowers your perception of the game and hence of your standard of play. The deal totals 53 tiles out of the 144 in the initial wall less the 14 tiles at the end of the wall, which are never used, an overall total of 130. The laws of probability dictate that at the start of play the collective holdings of the players average 13 tiles of each suit, five dragons, six winds and three bonus tiles. When replacements for the bonus tiles are drawn (assuming the average distribution), 56 tiles, that is 43% of the total, have already been distributed. On average, therefore, every tile in your hand that is not duplicated is likely to be matched in the hand of one or other of your opponents. This in turn means that the remaining pair of tiles are in the wall and that you have, at best, only a 50% chance of drawing one of them. And finally, allow in your calculations for the fact that the game is likely to end before all the tiles are drawn. Of course, this is rough planning only but it is important that you do not lose sight of the arithmetic involved. Probability is a better bet than possibility.

Initial assessment

You start by assembling your tiles on the rack. You should do this by picking them up and placing them at random. The temptation is to assemble the tiles in some kind of order and then to rearrange them. This should be avoided. Your actions may be observed by the other players (and they will certainly be monitored by experienced players) so already you will be giving information away. The message is caution. Any rearrangement that you wish to make should be conducted discreetly and preferably spread over a number of turns. In particular, avoid separating your hand into groups, for example by keeping sets or pairs apart. At the same time, you may profit from observing how your opponents are arranging their tiles, a legitimate ploy — mahjong is a cut-throat game!

You will need to start planning from the outset. First, examine the shape of your hand. Your aims will be three-fold; to go mahjong before the other players, to build, if possible, a high-scoring hand, and to hinder your opponents by disguising your intentions and by withholding tiles that they need. But be prepared to change your plan, perhaps many times, as events unfold. For now, however, you have only the tiles on your rack to guide you. Ultimately all will depend on what the opponents meld and discard and what you draw from the wall. At this stage though this is a blank page.

Sample hands

We will now look at a few opening hands and discuss their prospects. Here is a typical deal:

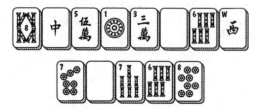

For ease of comment, let us put the tiles in some kind of order so that we can discuss the hand's potential:

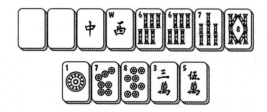

The two white dragons are a decided plus. If the two remaining white dragons are split, at the outset or later, as is likely, they are candidates for discards, so the prospects of a pung are good. Better, there is always the chance of drawing one or both of the remaining two from the wall for a concealed pung or kong. If, late in the game, no white dragons have appeared, it is quite likely that another player holds the remaining pair. All the more reason not to discard them. Retain them at all costs. Remember, they are a scoring pair in the final count. The other two honour tiles (red dragon and west wind) could be kept, at least for the time being, in the hope of drawing a second from the wall when your chance of being able to pung a discard would be greatly increased. But do not hold onto them for long. If possible, do not discard either until an identical tile has been discarded by another player. The hand has a chow of bamboos, valueless except as a step towards mahjong. The extra 6 of bamboos should be kept in the hope of making a pung and simultaneously abandoning the chow. A slight point in favour of the chow is that it is concealed — the other players cannot know of its existence. A melded pung on the other hand, although scoring, tells them that you are that much nearer mahjong.

The 7 and 8 of circles offer two chances of a chow — a 6 or a 9. The 3 and 5 of characters on the other hand offer only one chance (a 4 of characters). As an opening plan, your discards should therefore be in the order 1 of circles, which has no link to anything, and the 3 and 5 of characters with the west wind and red dragon in that order as possibles later. If, however, west is the wind of the round or you are sitting in the west seat, then west wind rates equally with the red dragon; and if west is both the prevailing wind and your seat, the red dragon should take precedence as a discard.

To repeat the warning above, you should be prepared to alter your strategy. For example, supposing two west winds are amongst the first few discards. Now the value of your wind has much diminished. All you could hope for would be a pair and the second tile would have to come from the wall, short of claiming it for mahjong. The chance of your drawing the tile would be roughly three to one against, and even then you would have no hope of a set. Accordingly, west wind should probably take priority over the red dragon as a discard.

Here is another hand that shows some promise:

First, you declare the two bonus tiles and draw two replacements. Already you are 8 points to the good. Suppose you now draw another green dragon (more luck!) and a 5 of bamboos. Again we will rearrange the tiles for ease of discussion:

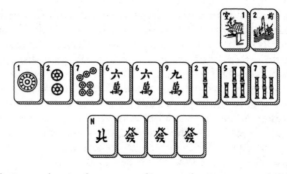

The obvious plus is the pung of green dragons, worth 8 points. Since the remaining green dragon will be of no use to the other players, there is a fair chance that it will be discarded early on when the holder is squeezed, and there is always the unlikely possibility that you will draw it from the wall. The pair of 6 of characters is a definite 'hold' in the hope of a pung or in its own right as a pair. The three bamboo tiles are worth keeping, at least for the time being. During the course of a balanced game you are likely to pick up two or three bamboo tiles. Any bamboo tile will now give you the chance of a chow and you could hope for better. The 1 and 2 of circles are not brilliant since only one tile — a 3 of circles — will complete a chow. The 7 of circles and the 9 of characters are potential discards. The north wind may also be a future discard but preferably not until another player has discarded one. It is difficult to foretell the final shape of the hand but two sets of bamboos seem quite likely. Where the rest of a mahjong hand is coming from is not immediately clear. A little more luck will be required.

The following hand is unusual:

At first glance it looks a random deal: not a pair or a potential pung or chow in sight. However, a second look reveals that the hand has nine different major tiles. Another four and this will be a limit hand, The Thirteen Unique Wonders. Admittedly, to draw three of the missing four tiles (east wind, the 1 and 9 of circles and the 1 of bamboos) from the wall (the last can be claimed from a discard) is going to require a lot of luck, but the stakes are high enough to warrant the risk, at least for the first few rounds. If you have agreed to score limit hands that are fishing, then this will be an added inducement to persevere. The message here is that when making an initial assessment of your tiles always be on the lookout for an embryo special hand.

Discards

The discards of the other players may have significance in two ways. Your opponents will sometimes discard tiles that you are able to claim and their discards will inevitably reveal information about their hands. Initially, of course, you have no idea what tiles your opponents have on their racks. Defensive planning at this stage is on hold. Defensive play is withholding the tile or tiles you believe the other players, and more particularly the player on your right who will be entitled to chow any of your discards, may want.

One of the most difficult skills in mahjong is remembering who discarded which tiles and, often of significance, in what order. As the game progresses this obviously gets harder. This is a similar skill to that required in Bridge where the strong player can recall all the cards played and who played them. However, the corresponding demand on the memory is much greater in mahjong. For one thing, there are more tiles than cards to remember, and for another there are four of each tile. The card player's ability to tick off mentally a specific card cannot be applied to a mahjong tile. Only very experienced players are able to keep a clear picture of what the other players have discarded and in what order. On the other hand, the mahjong player has one considerable advantage over the Bridge player: all discards are displayed throughout the game so that even a novice, hoping to complete a set, can easily check whether the tile he needs may still be available, and if so, what the odds are against getting it.

General hints

Pairs

If you have a pair and a discard gives you the opportunity for a pung, it may sometimes be best to decline it. The fourth tile, if held by another player now or later, will then be looked on as a safe discard and it may be better to take a chance and wait for this or, better still, a draw from the wall with a doubled point score, when you will be nearer completing your hand. There is always the risk that it will be part of another player's chow or languish in the wall but it is a chance that may be worth taking if you are going for a high-scoring hand. A melded pung is an indicator that you are on your way to mahjong and may prompt a player to go out early — for example, by falling back on chows — to frustrate you.

If you have a pair of 5 of bamboos for example and are hoping for a pung in order to go out, and you then draw a 6 of bamboos, what do you do? The answer will of course depend on exposed tiles (discards and melds), but in principle you should abandon the pair as you more than double your chances of a set, albeit a non-scoring one. You want an additional tile, of which there are only two, for the pung, whereas there may be anything up to eight tiles that will complete the chow. If, however, you draw a 7 of bamboos it is probably worth staying with the pair, other things being equal.

Too many pairs are bad for your health. Supposing you hold the following four pairs in your hand and are obliged to discard a tile. Which do you discard?

The correct answer is a tile from one of the central pairs. The remaining tile of the pair could be useful as part of a chow (4, 5, 6 or 5, 6, 7), whereas if you discard a tile from either of the end pairs you would be left with a single, worthless tile. It is a fact that it is easier to complete a pung when holding a pair than it is pairing a single tile. There is good reason for this. A matching tile for a pair must be drawn from the wall, whereas you have the additional chance of claiming a discard to complete a pung. A final word on pairs. Those that you hold should be committed to memory so that you do not overlook the chance of a pung.

Chows

If you are in a hurry to go mahjong and are happy to go out with a low-scoring hand, possibly because you fear another player is calling, the obvious strategy is to strive for chows. Apart from the precaution of checking discards and melds to ascertain your chances of drawing a wanted tile, there is one general rule that is worth remembering: terminals are of less use than simples. Consider the following three groups of tiles:

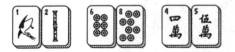

All three are potential chows but they are not all equal in value. In the first group only a 3 of bamboos will yield a chow; in the second, only a 7 of circles, but in the third there are two chances of a chow: a 3 or 6 of characters.

Improve your game

There are three attributes of the good player: concentration, patience and quickness of play. All are largely a matter of self-discipline; all will improve your game.

advanced strategy

In this chapter you will learn:
- when to attack and defend
- what to play and what not to play
- how to improve your hand.

The guidance offered in this chapter covers all forms of the game. This means that if you are playing the mainstream Chinese game, which is what this book is principally about, you will not be too concerned, for example, about one-suit hands, which are a feature of the cleared-hand game. In short, ignore any advice that appears to be irrelevant to the game you play. Experts concentrate almost entirely on the actions of the other players. Their superiority rests largely in their defensive play. Beginners on the other hand are inclined to concentrate on attack — the building of a mahjong hand. You should try to achieve a balance between the two. To a limited extent, some advice here is repeated. This is to emphasize important points.

You will need to adopt different strategies at different stages of the game as objectives change. A game can be divided into three phases: an opening phase — roughly the first six turns of play; a middle phase — roughly turns 7–12; and an end phase, after 12 turns of play if no player has by then gone mahjong. Below is some general advice in each of these phases divided into four parts covering: Hold — which tiles you should retain; Discard — those tiles you should dispose of; Attack — where you have a good hand and your aim is be the first to go mahjong; and Defence — where your prospects of going mahjong are thin and your aim is to hinder the other players. It is important to bear in mind, however, that these are general words of advice, not to be applied routinely as there will be occasions when they, or at least some of them, do not apply. In particular, you will often find yourself squeezed on discards where your only plausible choices are theoretically bad. In cases like this you must be guided by the current situation. Every hand of mahjong is in a sense unique.

Opening phase

Hold

General
Hold all pairs and sets, at least for the time being.

Honour tiles
Hold single tiles of dragons, own wind and prevailing wind. If you get a second from the wall you will have a scoring pair. Be alert to your seat direction and the wind of the round.

Remember that prevailing wind tiles are a bonus for everyone but your own wind is applicable only to you. If you have a bad hand, hold all dragons. If you hold one of each dragon, which is considered unlucky, experts rate this a signal to go on the defensive. Honours are attractive as they score when combined but they are harder to meld, whereas suit tiles are much easier since they can also be used to form chows.

Suit tiles

If you hold a lot of one suit it is likely that the opponents will discard them. Hold at least for the time being. If you have nine tiles of one suit, aim for a one-suit hand. Otherwise hold suit tiles numbered 3 to 7 (there is a proverb: 3s and 7s are hard to get) and in particular 4s, 5s and 6s as long as possible. If an opponent pungs 3s or 7s of your suit it will be difficult to achieve a one-suit hand. If you are holding a sequence of four (e.g. 5, 6, 7, 8 in a suit), do not chow but wait hopefully for a 5 or 8 from the wall to form a pair. Your eye (pair in a mahjong hand) should, if possible, be formed early and at this stage should not be converted into a pung.

Do not be in a hurry to claim chows and pungs — two sets in the same suit will be a warning to others. If you draw 8 or 9 tiles with promise of a mahjong hand (for example, two sets and a pair or four pairs) you are well placed to go mahjong first. If, as sometimes happens, you draw say 10 tiles towards a special hand your chances of making the hand are good but pay attention to your opponents' plays. For example, if you are aiming for Thirteen Unique Wonders and an opponent puts down a kong of green dragons the potential hand is destroyed.

Discard

General

Discarding a tile identical to one discarded by another player is generally sound, particularly if your discard is only a few turns after the other player. All you have to remember is that if it is a suit tile you may be giving a chow to the player on your right. At this stage of the game it is not too important.

Honour tiles

Decide at once what you are going to do with any dragons you draw — discard or hold. If you have one of each of the dragons and draw another to make a pair, discard the other two quickly. If you are in the east seat (and hence pay/receive double) discard dragons early or not at all. Discard all honour tiles early if you have a miserable hand with little chance of a mahjong. However, keep the wind of any skilful player but get rid of yours immediately if another is discarded. This is to minimize the chance of opponents punging. Winds are priority discards unless own/prevailing wind. First discard the wind you would least like to be claimed; next discard the wind of the player on your left. If he pungs you get another turn!

Suit tiles

Discard first from the weakest suit in the hand (single tiles) then terminals followed by 2s and 8s. Throw out less safe discards early. If you hold 1, 4, 7 in a suit discard the 1 first and later the 4. If you hold two consecutive tiles (e.g. 5, 6) there is no need to claim a discard for a chow (thereby revealing information to your opponents) as you should be able to draw a tile you want from the wall (eight possibilities). However, claiming a discard is not wrong if the set you form gives no indication as to the hand you are building.

Discard suit tiles 4, 5 and 6 last unless they are unlikely to be of use to you, when you should discard them early. Do not discard threes and sevens until the player on your right does so. If you discard a suit tile and your discard is chowed, avoid discarding that suit again.

An early discard of a simple by an opponent can mean that adjacent numbers of the suit are safe discards as discards early in the game tend to be isolated values.

Attack

General

You attack only if prospects for mahjong or a special hand look promising. Avoid early commitments if possible. Evaluate your hand and estimate the number of tiles required for mahjong. If you need four or fewer you are likely to be calling in under nine turns. It is seldom that any player is calling in the opening phase.

Honour tiles

If holding a pair of winds, it will probably be better to retain these as a pillow rather than promote to a pung and certainly if claiming a discard for the pung. If you have two red dragons and two east winds and an east wind is discarded, it may be better to duck this and wait for a red dragon and then claim the fourth east wind tile that will probably be discarded later. If you pung the first east wind it is likely that your opponents will hold up playing a red dragon.

Suit tiles

Do not collect the suit of your left-hand opponent since it is unlikely he will discard any. A hand of simples in one suit is fairly easy to make. If your hand is strong in 1s and 9s go for Heads and Tails. If holding a chow at the start go for an all-chow hand or melds of one suit. All limit hands require a strong opening hand to have any chance of success. With the right start, a hand of dragons, winds and terminals is not difficult to assemble.

An early chow based on a discard is poor play. It will deprive you of a good hand and discloses information. Also, do not make kongs too eagerly; it is often better to make a pung and keep the fourth tile for a chow. It may pay to go for an all-chow hand. Chows are much easier to get than pungs. If your suit tiles are a serial pair (e.g. 2, 3) there are eight tiles that will give you a chow, whereas with a pair of tiles there are only two tiles available for a pung.

Defend

General

You are on the defensive if you draw a bad hand (six or more single tiles) giving little prospect of mahjong. Do not give up: hands can change rapidly. There is a Chinese proverb: 'the player who becomes disheartened will lose everything'. If you draw five single tiles you might hope to be calling after 10 turns. In this case, combine defence and attack with the primary aim of not losing. A decision not to attempt mahjong at the start of a hand is one of the most important techniques in the game. Your strategy is to stop the other players going out by aiming for a wash-out or at least by keeping their scores to the minimum. Play defensively against the player on your right in particular. Players often combine to prevent East winning, since he is paid double. Do not pung or chow, as in this way you retain a maximum number of potential discards.

Honour tiles

Discard east wind tiles early, otherwise do not discard winds and dragons. If you have a pair of honours and one is discarded, do not pung but look on your pair as safe discards.

Suit tiles

The player to the left of East should ideally collect the same suit as East (check East's discards to discover what suit he is collecting). If you suspect that East has a strong one-suit hand, collect chows in the hope of being able to go out with a few lucky draws. Do not discard suit tiles 3, 4, 5, 6 and 7.

Middle phase

Hold

General

At this stage of the game you should have made a decision on whether to attack (go for mahjong) or defend (stop any of the other players going mahjong). If you have a weak hand but feel that you will not be able to stop someone going mahjong, cut your losses by stopping East if possible and assist the player who would appear to have the weakest hand or who perhaps is the weakest player. According to your chosen strategy you must decide what tiles you need to hold. A pair is always a good bet, particularly if the other two tiles have been discarded, since they are valuable if you are trying for mahjong and safe discards if you have gone on the defensive.

Honour tiles

If a player has two sets of dragons exposed, hold any tile of the remaining dragon and similarly withhold the fourth wind if a player has sets of the other winds exposed. If you are East and you hold two east winds and two west winds you should claim a discarded east wind for a pung but not a west wind, although you would probably reconsider if West were the prevailing wind. If, as East, you hold one each of north, south and west winds, discard in order of strongest to weakest player.

Suit tiles

In principle, collect the suit or suits that your left-hand opponent is not collecting. Again, hang on to 3s and 7s. Sequences of four or more tiles in the same suit often offer several ways of going out. They are particularly useful if no pair is held. The sequence 5, 6, 7, 8 will yield a pair and a chow if a 5 or 8 is drawn from the wall. A small point is that if you hold the 5 and 7 of a suit it is better to hold the 5 and discard the 7. Later, if you pick another 7 from the wall, the player on your left may consider the 6 a safe discard, giving you a chow.

Discard

General

The game is now going critical. You should, after six turns, have some idea of the other players' holdings, and in particular what suits they are probably collecting. Decide on a sequence of discards but be prepared to change it if events dictate. Do not claim a pung and even discard from a pung if you have but a solitary pair. The ideal discard is the fourth tile of another player's exposed pung, but it is seldom that you find yourself in this situation. A good general rule is to throw out the suits that your left-hand and opposite opponents appear to be collecting on the grounds that they will not be able to chow them.

If you discard a tile you picked from the wall, then it is obvious to the other players that your hand has not changed. Better to discard another tile from your hand or, if the tile you picked up is your best discard, juggle the tiles on your rack to deceive the opposition as to which tile you are throwing out.

Honour tiles

Winds and dragons are obviously safe discards if three of the same value are exposed or discarded. This is fairly easy to ascertain from discards; winds and dragons stand out amongst the suit tiles.

Discard a single dragon or wind if one of the same value is discarded. Do not hold onto two separate honour tiles. As North do not claim a pung from an East discard unless essential. The point here is that you would be giving East (who, remember, scores double) an extra turn.

Suit tiles

If everyone is discarding a suit, then no-one wants it. If on the other hand a suit is not being discarded, then it is probably being collected by more than one player. If a player is discarding circles and bamboos it may well mean that he is collecting characters. The reason good players tend to go for one-suit hands is that, by collecting a suit, you have a better chance of forming chows and pairs and even pungs than if your suits are fragmented. When going for a one-suit hand do not discard consecutive suit tiles on consecutive turns as this would indicate your intentions and at this stage of the game the suit you are collecting may then be all too apparent. A player is probably going for a one-suit hand if he discards two suits or two adjacent suit tiles.

If a player draws a tile, shows no interest in it and discards it, suit tiles adjacent or close to the one discarded should be safe discards, at least as far as that player is concerned. On the other hand, if a player shows an interest in a tile before discarding it he probably holds a closely related group.

Watch the player on your right (since he is the player who can chow your discards). If he throws a 1 of a suit, you can throw a 2 and if he throws a 9 or 7, then an 8 is a safe discard. Here there is a useful little formula known as the Rule of Three, particularly useful when an opponent is suspected of going for a one-suit hand or of course if the cleared-hand rule is in force. Study the following table:

$$1 - 4 - 7$$
$$2 - 5 - 8$$
$$3 - 6 - 9$$

You will see that in each line the numbers are three apart. Without going into the theory (which is a bit involved) the message is that if an opponent discards any suit tile, then an adjacent number in the table in the same suit is usually a safe discard. For example, the opponent you are most concerned about discards a 1 of circles, then a 4 should be a safe discard, and if he discards a 4, then a 1 and 7 are both fairly safe discards. A good rule of thumb!

Attack

General
Watch the faces of the other players: they can be very revealing in disclosing an interest or disinterest in a suit or tile. For your part, a little subterfuge may not go amiss – like showing an interest in a suit or tile in which you are not interested.

If you have a concealed pung in hand and the fourth tile is discarded, consider calling a pung and keeping the fourth tile in hand for a possible chow – remember, the tile can be played later for a kong if necessary. Always think whether you want to pung the first discard or to wait for the hoped-for second discard, but bear in mind that it might be sitting in the last 14 tiles.

Honour tiles
Do not pung an ordinary wind (that is, a wind that is not the prevailing wind or your seat wind) at the first opportunity – wait for the second discard.

Suit tiles

Do not pung a 3 if holding 1, 1, 2, 2, nor a 7 if holding 8, 8, 9, 9. Also, if holding 1, 2, 3, 3 do not pung a 3 as you have a chow and a 3 is now a safe discard. Similarly if holding 6, 6, 7, 8, for example, do not make a pung if a 6 is discarded for the same reason. If however you are fishing, then of course the discard of a 6 or 9 would allow you to go out. If you hold a sequence of four suit tiles with a gap and starting or ending in a terminal – for example, 1, 2, 4, 5 – and you pick the 3 from the wall or a discard, marry it with the 1, 2, not the 4, 5. Terminals are hard to get rid of and 4, 5 are central tiles and are more desirable. The advice for an ordinary wind (above) also applies to terminals – duck the first chance of a pung.

Defend

General

By the time you reach the ninth or tenth round you should have made up your mind as to whether to go for attack or defence.

Be prepared to sacrifice ruthlessly, breaking sets as necessary if squeezed for a safe discard. Before breaking a set decide which tile or tiles will make the safest discards. Generally speaking, kongs, pungs and chows in that order make the safest discards. Pairs should always be retained unless at least one of the value is exposed.

Honour tiles

Do not discard winds or dragons as at this stage another player may be fishing for a pair.

Suit tiles

Decide which is the safest suit to discard and remember that the player on your right can chow your discard.

End phase

Hold

General

The game is now down to the last section of the wall. The only reason you would hold back a tile at this stage of the game would be either because it enhances your prospects of going out or because the discard would be dangerous. After a dozen turns it is quite likely that at least one player is calling — the situation is turning critical and the stakes are high.

Clearly, the more tiles that would allow you to go out the better your chances. In this respect you should monitor the discarded tiles as well as those exposed on the other players' racks. If theory tells you that any of four different tiles would get you out and the tiles are already visible on other players' racks or among the discards you are going nowhere. By this stage you should be holding at least one pair 'for the eyes'. Only a discarded dragon or a bonus wind (own wind/wind of round) should be considered for a pung if you have no other pair. Supposing you have four sets and a single tile waiting for a companion. This is the worse situation to be in as your chances of getting a pair are thin indeed and the odds are on another player going mahjong first. If however you are seeking a single tile for a chow, you are no better off. If no tiles of the value you are seeking are exposed, then unless someone has a hidden kong (unlikely) or a hidden pung and a chow (not necessarily held by the same player) containing the desired tile (more likely but still odds against), the most likely case is that there is a hidden pung or a pair, which means that there is still a hidden tile or, as quite often happens, two players are sitting with pairs and it is unlikely that either player will discard from one.

If only one tile of the value you are seeking has been discarded, then the most likely situation is again that one player has a hidden pung or possibly a pair with the remaining tile in a chow. With two exposed tiles it is possible for one player to have the remaining two, which he is keeping as a pair. It depends when the discards were made: if recently, the situation is more promising as the holder of the pair did not take advantage of the pung. With three exposed tiles the singleton could be in a concealed chow or it could still be in the wall. Recall that a kong in hand only counts as a pung so declare it unless you have good reason not to (remember, it earns you a tile from the kong box that could be just what you want).

Honour tiles

Hold any wind or dragon you draw from the wall unless at least one, and preferably two identical tiles have already been discarded.

Suit tiles

If you have a mid-suit chow in hand and draw a sequential tile (example: you hold 5, 6, 7 and draw a 4), you should hold it, particularly if you lack a pair. Similarly if you have a run of four and draw a fifth (3, 4, 5, 6 and draw a 7), you should hold the 7.

If you have two adjacent pungs in the same suit (not a common occurrence admittedly) and you draw an adjacent tile (e.g. you have 5, 5, 5 and 6, 6, 6 of circles and draw a 4 of circles), this should be kept, giving you two chances for a pung, chow and pair.

Discard

General

A critical stage has now been reached and a casual discard could prove disastrous. (In some versions of the game, if a player goes mahjong on a discard then the discarder has to pay for all the losers.)

Sometimes you may be seeking to help a weak or low-scoring player to go out as a means of limiting your losses. Failing this situation, you will be looking above all for a safe discard. If the discard also misleads the other players as to your intentions, so much the better.

It might be argued that at this stage of the game there are few safe discards, and that almost all discards will carry at least a minimum risk. Monitor carefully exposed sets and the dead tiles. Avoid discarding any tile of which there are none visible. Discard the same tiles, where possible, as those discarded by the player you believe to be closest to going out.

If a player has three sets exposed be very careful what you throw out. If all three sets are in the same suit, do not discard any tile of that suit and if one set is of dragons avoid discarding any honour.

Honours

A safe discard is any honour of which three have already been played. It is true that it might be required for a special hand, but special hands are so rare that this can be discounted. However, unless three of a value are exposed, winds and dragons should not be discarded if drawn at this stage (odd honour tiles should have been discarded earlier: any retained should continue to be retained).

In particular, the third dragon should never be discarded if a player already has two sets of dragons, and the fourth wind is taboo as a discard if a player is showing sets of the other three winds.

If you have an incomplete one-suit hand with a pair of honour tiles, it may prove to be a good gamble to discard the honours in the hope of achieving a high-scoring one-suit hand.

Suit tiles

No suit tile can ever be truly safe, if only because it could form part of a chow. However, as a chow can be claimed only by the player on your right, the risk is much reduced. Keep the safest discards as late as possible; it is too easy to reach a stage where you may have no alternative but to throw down a dangerous tile.

If you have been following the opponents' plays carefully you should have a good idea by now what suits they have been collecting. Terminals are good discards but not if a player is showing three sets of them. Next, twos and eights are good discards. Discard a pair of simples rather than two consecutive values. If forced, a pung can be safely thrown out. It has the advantage of giving three safe discards.

Suppose now that you are striving for mahjong and you have three sets, a pair and 1, 3, 5 of a suit. Prefer the 1 as a discard with the 5 as the alternative, never the middle value. Three-tile combinations are worth absorbing. Given 2, 4, 4, (or similar, excluding terminals), discard the 2; if 1, 2, 4 discard the 1. If your random tiles are 6, 7, 7, 9 wait to pung the 7s; discard the 6 as you are more likely to get a 9 than a 6 to form a pillow.

Suppose you hold 1, 1, 3, 3, 4, 5, 5 where the 1s and 3s could also be honour tiles and you are given the chance of a pung. Take it, but be careful of your discard. If the 1s or 3s are punged, discard a 5, not a 4 as there is a much better chance of a chow than a pung of 5s.

Attack

General

A good ploy at this stage is to delay the declaration of a concealed kong. In order to go mahjong of course you will need to declare it sooner or later. There is a risk involved: if someone goes mahjong it will only count as a pung. However, it is possible that another player, who is perhaps calling, wants the tile for a chow. If you declare the kong as soon as you draw the fourth tile, that other player will see at once that his strategy is faulty and switch objectives. Another trick: declare three tiles for a pung but hold back the fourth. You then retain three options for the single tile: you can declare a kong later, you can use it in a chow or even discard it.

Honour tiles

Recall that a pair of honour tiles will earn you points so if left with an honour and a suit tile and there are equal chances of either coming up, discard the suit tile.

Suit tiles

With three sets and a pair, a chow is usually the quickest way to mahjong. It is an obvious aim for East, who will collect double from the other players, but it is also a target for all the players.

Certain situations militate against a kong. Supposing you have four tiles left to meld: 7, 7, 7, 8 and need a pair. You now draw the fourth 7. What do you do? If you declare a kong and draw a replacement tile from the kong box the chances are that you will be left with two unmatched tiles. After your discard you will be left with a single tile to pair — the worst possible scenario. Instead of making the kong you should discard a 7, maintaining the status quo. Now you need a 6 or 9 to go out (chow and pair). If you did not have a sequential tile — say you had 5, 5, 5, 8, and drew the fourth 5 — then there would be no virtue in not declaring the kong, as there is no embryo chow. And at least you would get a second chance to match the 8 with a draw from the kong box.

Defend

General

The game is now close to the finishing line and you may only get another couple of turns. The decision when to go over from attack to defence is a difficult one. It is a skill that marks the expert from the amateur. It comes down to calculating the odds objectively, taking full account of the number of tiles remaining in the live wall. It is at this stage in the game that many players will be under tension and may reveal valuable information by their handling of the tiles, facial expressions and body movements. Watch closely. For example, a player who is fishing frequently reveals this by closely examining the discards and exposed hands to determine how many chances he has of getting the tile he wants. The experts also say that a player who is calling will straighten his back, revealing that the tension of the game is over and all that is required now is to wait for the right tile. Under these circumstances your aim will be to go out as quickly as possible, and failing that to deny the player a tile you think he may want, even if this means breaking a set.

Be careful about declaring a kong near the end of a game: you could be 'robbed' (see Robbing the Kong). Be ruthless: if you have a tile or tiles that you know another player wants (all players should by now be close to mahjong and an observant player will have a good idea of who has been collecting what) and have no other obvious discards, break one of your own concealed sets. Good players do this frequently. If you believe a high-scoring hand is close to mahjong feed a lower-scoring player to minimize your losses. A sound strategy is to frighten another player into going mahjong so as to limit your losses. If the live wall is nearly exhausted and you are not calling, play for a draw by discarding safe tiles even if that means wrecking your own prospects.

Honour tiles
At this stage of the game, retain honour tiles at all costs unless clearly safe to discard.

Suit tiles
Do not claim a chow unless you are on the point of going out. The set is worth nothing; it is an indication to the other players. A better play is to draw from the wall. Retain 3s and 7s, even if it means breaking up one of your sets.

Calling
When you need only one tile to go mahjong you are said to be calling. This is also termed 'fishing', 'waiting' or 'ready'. This does not mean that you can now afford to sit back and stop thinking. Your chance of drawing a particular tile will depend on how many tiles of the same value are still in the wall or have not yet been declared. However, you are more likely to get the tile you want from a discard, rather than from the wall — there are three discards for every tile you draw. The best chance, if you are waiting for one tile, is that two or three matching tiles are still available. But if none is visible at this stage it is more than likely that another player has a pung, or at least a pair of

them. You should consider, therefore, that the tile you have just drawn from the wall may give you a better chance than the single tile in hand. The fact is that with a single tile to match, your chances of going mahjong are far from healthy.

The skilful player plans the hand at an early stage aiming for the largest number of chances possible. One way to achieve this is to collect a single suit. This will probably be governed by the deal. If you draw, say, seven or eight of the same suit at the outset you are well on your way. With one hand, Gates of Heaven, any one of nine tiles will yield mahjong. It applies to a single-suit hand only:

In this concealed hand any character tile will let you go out. If you drew a 1, 4 or 7 you could go out with a pair of 9s; if a 2, with a pair of 2s; if a 3, 6 or 9 with a pair of 1s; finally a 5 would give you a pair of 5s and an 8 a pair of 8s. Now admittedly the chance of finding yourself in this happy position is remote. However, many hands can offer a multiple choice of tiles for mahjong and obviously the larger number of chances at your disposal the better. This is often not a matter of chance but one of planning. The following tile distributions are to be aimed for; obviously the larger the number of chances they offer the better. Similar combinations are also valid, for example any two consecutive simples give two chances, but chances are reduced in many cases if terminals are included. Numbers refer to tiles of the same suit.

One chance	Single tile
Two chances	6, 7 — go out with 5 or 8
	1, 1, 1, 2 — go out with 2 or 3
	8, 9, 9, 9 — go out with 7 or 8
Three chances	3, 4, 5, 6, 7 — go out with 2, 5 or 8
	2, 3, 4, 5, 6, 7, 8 — go out with 2, 5 or 8
	6, 6, 6, 7 — go out with a 5, 7 or 8
	1, 1, 6, 6, 6, 7, 8 — go out with 1, 6 or 9
Four chances	4, 4, 5, 5, 6, 6, 6 — go out with 3, 4, 5, or 6
	3, 4, 5, 6, 6, 6, 7 — go out with 2, 5, 7 or 8

Five chances	3, 4, 5, 6, 7, 7, 7 — go out with 2, 3, 5, 6 or 8	
Six chances	2, 2, 2, 3, 3, 3, 4, 5, 6, 7 — go out with 2–5, 7 or 8	
Seven chances	1, 1, 1, 2, 3, 4, 5, 6, 6, 6 — go out with any 1–7	
	4, 4, 4, 5, 6, 7, 8, 9, 9, 9 — go out with any 3–9	
Eight chances	2, 2, 2, 3, 4, 5, 6, 7, 7, 7 — go out with any 1–8	
	3, 3, 3, 4, 5, 6, 7, 8, 8, 8 — go out with any 2–9	

Most of the above tile combinations are improbable. Suppose though you have four tiles all of the same suit and, instead of thinking in terms of values, as in the above table, you think more realistically in terms of numbers. So for example the combination 6, 7 above allows you to go out with two values, either the 5 or the 8. This can be translated into eight tiles less any that form part of sets in hand or are exposed in opponents' sets or in discards. On the same basis of numbers rather than tile values, the following combinations of four tiles of the same suit vary between two and 11 chances less the number of tiles exposed or are elsewhere in your hand. Thus in the first example below one tile only will do: a 5, and there are only two chances to go out (as you hold two 5s already).

	Possibilities	*Chances*
4, 5, 5, 6	1	2
4, 4, 6, 8	1	4
4, 4, 6, 6	2	4
4, 5, 6, 7	2	6
4, 4, 5, 6	2	6
4, 4, 4, 6	2	7
1, 2, 2, 2	2	7
4, 4, 7, 8	2	8
4, 4, 4, 5	3	11

Improving your hand

You are calling. There are two ways in which you can improve your hand at this stage. One is by increasing your chances of going out and the other is by increasing the value of your holding. In the latter case, do not overlook the possibility of earning a double. Going out, however, is invariably more important than just getting a few extra points. It is here that the inexperienced player, who rarely overlooks a chance to complete a set, particularly a pung or a kong, is liable to fall down. Using the above table as an indicator, if you have two pairs — say 3, 3 and 5, 5 — and you draw a 6 from the wall,

all other things being equal you should hold the 6 and discard a 5 as you then have four more chances (8 against 4) of acquiring the tile you want. There are two sound general rules for the calling player with a single tile: a terminal or wind on the whole offers the best chance of a matching discard together with any tile that appears to have little value; for example, if pungs of the 6 and the 8 of bamboos are showing, a 7 of bamboos is a possible discard since it is unlikely to be needed for a chow. Overriding the above advice is the need of course to count how many of the tiles you want are showing, and if none are, consider the possibility that they form part of a concealed set or pair.

The expert, who is always alert to maximize his chances of going out, not infrequently declines a discard that would complete a set. A few examples follow. Correct handling of these and similar situations will greatly improve your play. The message is simple: make the play that will give you the most chances to go mahjong.

A warning: in your calculations always take account of exposed tiles — you should now be in the habit of monitoring them constantly. There is no point in electing for an option in which the tile or tiles you want have already been played. Even if one or more have been exposed this will of course reduce your chances.

In the following examples, let us assume that you have a couple of pungs, either exposed or concealed. You are faced with discarding from the following eight tiles. How do you maximize your chances?

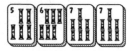 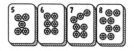

Discard a 7 of bamboos. Now a 5 or 8 of circles will give you mahjong. You could also discard the 5 or 8 of circles when you would be calling for a 4 or 7 of bamboos, but this might be pushing your luck as you have two 7s already. A good time to check what tiles have gone.

Another example. You have the following hand when the left-hand player discards a 6 of characters. What do you do?

If you are hasty, you might well be tempted to claim a pung and discard one of the two remaining characters. But this would be something of a disaster as it would leave you two tiles short of mahjong. Far better to forego the couple of points, claim the discard for a chow and discard the 3 of bamboos, giving you two chances to go out (the 4 and 7 of bamboos).

With the following hand you draw a 7 of circles. What do you discard?

Keep it and discard a 7 of characters. Now, instead of waiting for a single tile (the 7 of characters to give you two chows and a pair) you are waiting for the 4 or 7 of circles — two chances.

In this next example, you have three sets and just need a fourth set and a pair. You hold these tiles:

If a 3 of bamboos is thrown out by your left-hand opponent, do not claim the chow since after discarding you will be left with either a 2 or a 4 to match. Instead, if you draw from the wall you will in effect have another turn and furthermore either a 2 or a 4 will give you mahjong.

Do not always jump at triplets. In this last example you again have three sets and hold:

Now you draw a 1 of circles. What do you play? Discard it. At the moment you have two chances to go out: a 4 or 7 of characters, with up to eight tiles available. If you make a pung then you will have to discard either the 5 or 6 leaving yourself with the need to match the remaining tile — at most three tiles available.

09

mahjong for two, three, five or six players

Four players are not essential for mahjong. The game can be played by any number up to six and probably more. None of these arrangements is entirely satisfactory when compared with the four-player game, but at least they cater for those occasions when an odd number is required. The variants deviate little from the basic game and then mostly in the preliminaries rather than the play. In all games players start with an agreed number of tallies (2,000 is popular).

Mahjong for two players

This is a very useful game for beginners who wish to acquire a basic knowledge of the rules, management of the hand, scoring and settlement, whilst avoiding the often intimidating procedures of the full game, and in particular the complex strategy associated with it. The minimum requirement laid down for going mahjong ensures that games will be sufficiently protracted to enable the players to analyze their hands and to adjust their plans as circumstances change. The players have only to monitor the discards of one opponent, and further to simplify this, they can agree to keep their discards apart from each other and also, if desired, to place the discarded tiles in rows so that the order in which they were thrown out can be readily seen.

The two players are East and West and they sit opposite each other. East rolls two dice to decide which wall will be broken and then rolls them again, adding the total to the first roll to determine where the wall is broken. The deal is as in the basic game with East drawing the extra tile and then starting play by discarding. Usually the game is played with the stipulation that chows are not allowed except in a limit hand and, further, a player may not go mahjong without four or more doubles, with doubles for bonus tiles, if used, not counting. The four-double rule is useful practice since it familiarizes the players with the science of doubling, which often means that a pung or even a kong may have to be broken in order to acquire the necessary minimum of doubles. Scoring is exactly as in the four-player game but settlement is different. The player with the lower-scoring hand pays the opponent the point difference. Notice that in this version East does not pay or receive double. Players take it in turns to roll the dice at the start of each hand or, an alternative arrangement, when West wins a hand he becomes East and so on.

Mahjong for three players

There are two mainstream games, one using the regular square wall and the other a triangular wall. There is little to choose between them. In the four-sided game, the north wind position is vacant and is termed Dummy. (If, in the preliminary stage, North is called on to roll the dice or break the wall, the functions are performed by West.) There are three hands in each round. When West loses his hand, the deal reverts to East (i.e. there is no north hand). If it is agreed to allow chows, East may claim a West discard. Some three-handed games are played over four rounds but three rounds are more logical with the players rotating wind positions after each round. Scoring and settlement are as for the four-player game but if chows are disallowed (a common prohibition), except in special hands, there is no double for a no-chow hand. This is the recommended game for three players but one or other of the versions that follow may be preferred. In one, the winds are treated as dragons, of which there are now four rather than three, and the dragons become winds thus: green = east wind, red = south wind and white = west wind. Scoring is adjusted accordingly. A different version has the north wind tiles treated as bonus tiles and a Japanese version has the north wind tiles as an extra dragon.

If a goulash is played, the player exchanging tiles with Dummy first sets aside three tiles from his own hand and then picks three tiles unseen from anywhere in the live wall, replacing them with the three he set aside.

The game using three walls instead of four eliminates the north position. The north wind tiles and the bonus tiles familiar to north (winter and bamboo) are set aside, reducing the number of tiles to 138. The walls are thus of 23 stacks (46 tiles) and are pushed together to form a triangle. Play then proceeds as in the four-player game. There are three hands in each round and three or four rounds, as agreed, in a game. In another three-wall version, the north winds and all bonus tiles are omitted and each wall comprises 22 stacks (44 tiles), otherwise the game is the same. In Malaysia and Singapore the three-player game is sufficiently popular to justify the marketing of triangular mahjong tables.

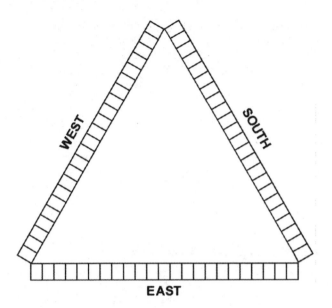

the triangular wall

An American system that includes the bonus tiles builds three walls, whilst the fourth wall (36 tiles) is distributed evenly between the players (12 tiles each) and the remaining tiles of the deal (two for East, one for each of the other players) are drawn from the live wall as for a deal.

In all the three-wall versions it is possible to play a goulash. This takes place immediately following the deal. East passes three tiles face down to South, who simultaneously passes three tiles to West, who at the same time passes three tiles to East. In the second round, the sequence is reversed: East passes to West, who passes to South, who passes to East. A second goulash can then be played if desired.

Mahjong for five players

This is fairly uncomplicated with one player sitting out each hand. Initially one tile of each of the four winds, together with a dragon tile (usually white or red) are shuffled face down and the players draw for seats. The player who picks the dragon (who is sometimes known as the Dreamer) sits out for the first hand. The other players take their seats according to the tiles they

drew. Procedures, play and settlement is normal. East retains his
seat until he loses a hand, when he becomes the new Dreamer.
Now South becomes East, West is South, North is West and the
player who sat out comes in as North. The game proceeds in this
manner. A round is of five hands, each player having played in
four of them. A game is of four rounds, as usual. According to
one source, the Dreamer is paid by the others on completion of
a hand. He receives 2 points from each player, doubled as many
times as there are doubles in the winner's hand. Thus if the
winner went mahjong with three doubles, the Dreamer would
receive 16 points from each player, including the winner. This
additional payment is not recommended as it merely
complicates the settlement.

Mahjong for six players

Two suit tiles, the 1 and 9, are shuffled face down with one each
of the four winds. Each player draws a tile and the players who
drew the suit tiles sit out in the first game, the other players
taking their places according to the winds they drew. After the
first hand, East retires, regardless of the result. The South player
is the new East and the player who drew the 1 comes in as
North. Thereafter East retires at the end of each hand and the
player who has sat out longest comes in as North.

10
American mahjong

In this chapter you will learn:
- the cleared-hand game
- the one-double game
- about US organizations.

America was the first Western country to embrace mahjong where it achieved an instant popularity. There the game saw a cycle of change and experiment and to talk even today of one game as being American mahjong is as inaccurate as it is to talk of a single Chinese or Japanese version of mahjong. What is certain, however, is that it is in America that the game has always found the most support outside the Far East and it is probably nearly as popular there today as at any time since the heyday of the mid-1920s. So keen was business in the early boom years that if a tile was lost or damaged one of the replacement tiles that came with the sets could be sent to Shanghai, where it would be hand engraved and returned — free and post free!

At first the Chinese game was simplified, probably to give it mass-market appeal, but then there was pressure for adornments to meet the demands of an increasingly sophisticated public. Here were born many 'special hands', which passed for skill and met with popular approval at the time. A consortium of five experts drafted the American Official Laws of Mah-Jongg in 1924. But time was running out. The rise in popularity of contract bridge, the natural decline that follows any craze, and the proliferation of changes and special hands that led to confusion and irritation, together contributed to the decline of the game.

Cleared-hand game

Around this time American mahjong incorporated the idea of the '**cleared-hand**' and the '**one-double**' game. The cleared-hand game required that the player going mahjong could include only tiles of one suit plus honour and bonus tiles. No tile of the other two suits was permitted except in a limit (special) hand. The game had the disadvantage that during play it soon became rather obvious as to which suit each player was collecting. It also had other disadvantages. The first grounded set of suit tiles confirmed a player's chosen suit, whilst most tiles drawn from the wall were useless. Between experts, cleared-hand games tended to end in draws. Also, with four players and only three suits, two players at least must be collecting the same suit and are accordingly penalized. Here is a typical 'cleared hand' that has made mahjong:

One-double game

In the 'one-double' game, the mahjong player had to have at least one double in his hand before going out. The cleared hand (above) qualified for one double as it is limited to one suit. Here is a 'one-double' hand with mixed suits.

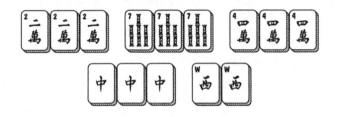

A double is awarded for a pung of dragons. The object of the 'one-double' hand was that it made it a little more difficult to go mahjong and was arguably more skilful. However, the game is still restrictive, limiting the player's choice. In the cleared-hand and one-double games there was no prohibition on using the last 14 tiles. The game was a draw only when the entire original wall was exhausted.

The National Mah Jongg League

In a praiseworthy effort to introduce some degree of uniformity into the American game, The National Mah Jongg League was formed in 1937. The modern mahjong set sold in America comprises 152 tiles, often with eight spares, a total of 160 tiles. The set consists of the basic 108 suit tiles, the 28 honour tiles, eight flowers and eight jokers, the latter of a uniform design. The League publishes an annual list of some 50 or so hands that qualify as mahjong together with the points (cents, in money terms) that each hand earns. All hands are made up of the conventional 14 tiles but no account is taken of the traditional requirement for four sets and a pair, whilst the humble chow is eliminated altogether. All qualifying hands are in effect special hands and have to be re-learnt each year as the annual list automatically supersedes that of the previous year. About two-thirds of the designated hands are exposed hands, that is to say, they can include discards. Scoring is simplified. The points awarded for a hand vary between 25 and 60.

Two features distinguish the American game: the introduction of jokers and the Charleston (also known as the Razzle). In the League game there are eight jokers. A joker may be substituted for any tile, and furthermore if exposed may be claimed by another player, who exchanges it for the tile that it represents. The availability of jokers admits multiple-tile sets, in theory, up to 14 tiles (seven flowers and seven jokers representing flowers) but in practice mainly confined to quints (sets of five).

The Charleston

This is a procedure, widespread in America, designed to disturb the initial distribution of tiles to the extent of permitting players to improve their hands before play begins. The Charleston also mitigates the boredom sometimes associated with the early rounds of play when hands tend to lack shape. It allows players to exchange unwanted tiles in order to advance their holdings towards one or other of the combinations that constitute the published mahjong hands. Without the Charleston and without the presence of jokers, most games would undoubtedly end in wash-outs.

After the deal, each player exchanges three tiles with each of the other players in a strict sequence. First, each player passes three unwanted tiles face down to the player on the right. Thus East would pass to South, South to West and so on. All players must place their tiles on the table before passing. Next, players exchange three tiles in the same manner with the player opposite and finally a third exchange takes place with the player on the left. On the last pass, any player may elect to pass unseen one, two or all three of the tiles received from the player on the right. This is known as a blind pass and its purpose is to permit a player to retain a promising hand without being compelled to pass tiles.

A second Charleston may now take place if all players agree. The order of passing is changed. The first pass is to the player on the left, the second to the player opposite and the third to the player on the right. Again, a blind pass is permitted on the final turn. Jokers may not be passed in a Charleston but flowers and seasons, collectively known as flowers in America, may be. (In some circles the Charleston takes place after all players have declared their bonus tiles.)

Under League rules flowers are part of the hand and attract no bonuses. The tiles are not numbered and so are unrelated to seating. Another feature of American mahjong is that the dragons are linked to suits as follows:

red dragon — characters
green dragon — bamboos
white dragon — circles.

Some special hands call for zeros that are represented by white dragons. The authorized mahjong hands would be difficult and in many cases impossible to achieve without jokers. Here are three League-authorized hands:

①

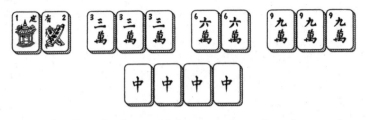

The numbers on the flowers (absent on most American sets) are ignored: any two flowers are valid in this hand. Notice that the kong of dragons is consistent with the suit (red dragons — characters). This hand can include exposed sets. It is worth 25 points.

②

The sets of dragons are interchangeable (for example, the pair could be green dragons) and again the flowers are in any combination. The hand can include exposed sets. It is worth 30 points.

③

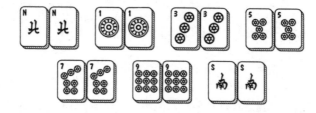

The suit pairs are all odd numbers and of the same suit. The hand must be concealed, except for the last tile, which may be a discard. It is worth 45 points.

There are only four doubles in the League game: if the player draws the winning tile from the wall, the other players pay double the value of the hand. If the hand is completed with a discard, the discarder pays double, the other players pay single. If a player completes a hand from the wall without jokers, all players pay four times the total; if from a discard, the discarder pays four times and the other two players twice the value of the hand. (There are one or two exceptions in this case.) There is no general settlement: only the player who goes mahjong is paid and East does not pay or receive double. Players initially receive chips (tallies) worth 1000 points. Chips are in four values: 200, 100, 25 and 5 points.

It will be seen that the League game is very different from the Chinese or European games, which is not to say that it does not have advantages. Its attraction lies in the novelty of the designated hands, the excitement of the Charleston, the scope for unusual and dramatic play made possible by the use of jokers, and the rationalized scoring system. Its popularity is testimony to its appeal.

The American Mah-Jongg Association

The American Mah-Jongg Association was formed in 1999 and has made big strides since then. The game played is as close to the League game as makes no difference but flexibility of rules is encouraged. The Association publishes an annual card of hands similar to the League card but the hands tend to be more innovative. Here are two of them taken from the 2001 card:

This all-pair hand, given a little imagination, reads FRIENDS with each letter doubled. (R is for red dragon, D for any dragon.)

②

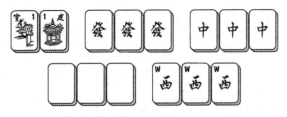

This traditional exposed hand (four sets and a pair) can be interpreted as FLOWERS GROW. (Here the white dragons represents a letter O rather than a zero.)

The Association hands for 2001 range in value from 25 to 100 (one dollar). Hands and values are subject to annual change as is the case with the League hands.

The Wright-Patterson Group

Another, very different school of American mahjong is espoused by the Wright-Patterson Group, with origins pre-Second World War. Although well established, it does not command the following of the League. Its appeal is more to the traditional player. The Wright-Patterson rules are largely those of Babcock's mahjong in 1920s America and hence close to the European game of today that has changed little over the years. For example, the set is made up of the usual 136 tiles plus the flowers and seasons that are treated as bonus tiles. There are no jokers and the scoring of hands, including doubles, is orthodox. The game ends in a wash-out if the live wall is exhausted. The kong box is inviolate but if this is exhausted in play, replacement tiles may be drawn from the end of the live wall. In one significant respect the Wright-Patterson game is in line with modern American tradition: the Charleston is performed at the start of each hand (after the bonus tiles have been declared and replacements drawn). However, unlike in the League game, there is no second bite at the cherry: there is only one Charleston. The Wright-Patterson game is also true to the American enchantment with special hands. It offers almost 100 of these as though there were virtue in numbers. They must surely tax the memory of even the most committed player. Here are a couple:

①

This orthodox-looking hand comprises a pung of red bamboos, a pung of green bamboos, a pung of both red and green dragons and a pair of white dragons. The hand is known as Christmas Eve and is worth double the limit.

②

This hand comprises pungs of 3s, 5s and 7s, all in the same suit, a pung of corresponding dragons and one each of the other two dragons. This hand is known as Chinese New Year and is worth a single limit.

The game conforms to the old mahjong when it comes to settlements. After the winner is paid (East as usual receiving/ paying double) the other players settle between themselves. As in some other versions of mahjong, Wright-Patterson offers that curious anomaly of double and triple limit awards.

All the above organizations run tournaments, publish rule books and newsletters, and market mahjong merchandise. Their other activities include arranging mahjong holidays and cruises. Two have websites that are well worth visiting.

National Mah Jongg League
250 West 57th Street
New York
NY 10107
website: www.nationalmahjonggleague.org

American Mah-Jongg Association
1330 Reisterstown Road
Lower Level, Suite 7
Baltimore
MD 21208
website: www.amja.ne

OWC Mah Jongg
Wright-Patterson AFB OWC
P.O. Box 67
Fairborn
OH 45324

Japanese mahjong

In this chapter you will learn:
- the history of mahjong in Japan
- Japanese terms and their meanings
- about the Mahjong Museum.

Mahjong reached Japan in the first decade of the twentieth century but the game made little impact until the mid-1920s, which saw the establishment of the first mahjong house. By 1929 there were over 1500 mahjong clubs in Tokyo alone, but these suffered a sharp decline with the introduction of anti-gambling laws.

The rules of play were regulated in the mid-1960s and resulted in a second boom that peaked a few years later. Today there are a number of mahjong organizations in Japan in which the game is played to slightly different rules. Mahjong remains immensely popular with a claimed 20 million players in the country, amongst them many of the world's strongest. The Japanese game (if one can talk of it as a single game with a single set of rules) has similarities and also marked differences with modern American mahjong (again used in a collective sense). It is a usual requirement that a player cannot go mahjong unless he has one fan (double; Chinese faan), which is the equivalent of the old American one-double game.

However, if he has a worthless hand, known as pinfu, which consists of chows only with a non-honour pair, the final tile from a discard, he may call mahjong. The reward is usually a modest 10 points for mahjong, doubled. Players often try for a fully concealed hand, which permits taking a discard for the last tile, as it scores extra.

Japanese mahjong may be described as a pattern-forming game, although it retains a large part of its Chinese ancestry. For example, special hands are mostly identical to those of the classical game, although scoring is subject to variation. There is also conformity in that the 14 tiles at the end of the wall are considered dead. One pattern not found in the Chinese game is the mixed pung. This is made up of three tiles of the same value, one from each suit. This set understandably cannot be extended to a kong.

a mixed pung

A popular scoring pattern (which is not of course a complete hand) is three sequences of identically-numbered tiles.

three sequences of identical-numbered tiles

In the 1920s the bonus tiles (flowers and seasons) were dropped from the game and later the all-pay-all system was replaced in favour of a single winner. The player who goes mahjong is paid by the other players who do not settle amongst themselves. East pays and receives double, as in the Chinese game. The effect of this is a faster game as going out is all-important as there are no rewards for high-scoring hands that fail. The Japanese also introduced a rule in the 1930s that the player who discards the winning tile has to pay for the other players, a harsh penalty where the player going mahjong has a concealed hand. The rule has the natural effect of making players extremely cautious when discarding. This, in turn, raises the standard of play since it compels players to monitor closely their opponents' plays.

Having dispensed with the bonus tiles, the Japanese introduced new bonus tiles that are scored differently. These include dora (which means 'gong') and red fives. In the case of dora, when the walls are built the dealer turns over the top tile three stacks from the end of the live wall. This tile is called the dora indicator. Dora is now established as the next tile in sequence to the dora indicator. By sequence is meant the next number above if a suit tile (for example, a 4 of circles is turned over; dora is the 5 of circles). Suit tiles are circular so that if a 9 is revealed, dora is a 1 of that suit. The honour tiles also run in circles thus: winds run E→S→W→N→E and dragons white→green→ red→ white. Every dora in a winning hand earns one double; however, a dora may not be used to meet the one-double minimum rule for mahjong. Red fives are usually three in number, one of the fives in each of the three suits that is daubed with red or otherwise distinguished. Every red five in a mahjong hand earns a double, as with dora, and equally cannot be used for the one-double minimum requirement.

A player who is calling is said to be ready — **riichi** is the term used. The player announces riichi, places his hand face down to indicate that he will not change it, and puts a 100 point bone on top of it. If he succeeds in going mahjong the other players pay him double and if he does not the player going mahjong appropriates it. An alternative rule to this awards one double to the riichi player who succeeds in going mahjong.

There is a rule known as the **Sacred Discard (fu)**. This states that a player cannot go mahjong with a tile identical to one that he has previously discarded. If, however, he needs either of two or more tiles to go out and one of these is a sacred discard, there is no restriction on going mahjong with a tile other than the sacred discard. There is no difficulty in determining the sacred discard as players are obliged to keep their discards face up in front of them in an orderly line so that it is not only possible to determine who discarded what, but also exactly on what turn a particular tile was discarded. This practice is crucial to the game as it allows players to avoid unwise discards.

Japanese mahjong recognizes a number of draws that are in effect abortive hands. These hands are in addition to the washout (exhaustion of live wall) that is of fairly frequent occurrence.

Five such abortive draws are admitted:

1 If, on the first round of discards, all players discard the same wind tile and no sets have been declared, play ends and the game is a draw.
2 If a player on his first turn and after drawing a tile has no set but has nine different honour tiles, he may expose his hand, whereupon the game is drawn.
3 If a total of four exposed kongs are declared, the game is a draw. This seems a curious rule.
4 If three players claim the same discard in order to go mahjong, the game is drawn and no payments are made.
5 If all four players have declared riichi, and the claims have been verified, the game is abandoned immediately.

The Mecca for mahjong players world-wide is the Mahjong Museum founded in 1999 at Misaki-cho near Tokyo. Apart from an impressive array of beautiful hand-crafted sets it houses over 10,000 documents relating to the game and its predecessors together with all manner of artifacts and equipment used in the manufacture of tiles. A handsome coffee-table book printed throughout in full colour illustrates some 200 of the museum's remarkable sets together with many other mahjong-related treasures housed in the museum. The text is in three languages, including English.

The Mahjong Museum
Take Shobo Co.
2–7–3 Iidabashi
Chiyoda-ku
Tokyo 102-0072

12

other variant forms

In this chapter you will learn:
- the common rule variations
- the modern Chinese game
- other variant forms.

There are a number of popular variants of the basic game that place restrictions on the composition of mahjong hands. The development of these variants came from a desire to adapt to regional preferences coupled with a perceived need to 'improve' the game by making it more interesting in the opinion of the innovators. Common restrictions are to curb the use of chows and also to forbid hands of mixed suits on the reasonable hypothesis that chows and mixed suits make the composition of a mahjong hand too easy and do not allow time for players to assemble interesting hands. This, in turn, means that high-scoring and special hands are at the least very difficult and in many cases near impossible to achieve. Social mahjong allows you to experiment with these restrictions if you are so inclined. Here, reduced to essentials, are variants that are worth an airing:

The bonus tiles are omitted Bonus tiles are pure chance having no part in the play but their artistic designs are appealing and they add a touch of glamour to the game. However, bonus tiles can add significantly to the value of a hand and they do influence the play. For example, a player may reject the chance to make a chow in favour of drawing from the wall in the hope of getting a bonus tile. One variation designed to limit the impact of these tiles on the play is by adding bonus points to a hand after the doubles (if any) have been executed. Another suggestion is to reduce their value to 2 points each with 8 points for own flower and season instead of one double. Serious players, however, object to bonus tiles altogether and in many parts of the world these are no longer used. If these tiles are omitted the walls are built of 17 stacks instead of 18.

Only one suit is allowed in a mahjong hand in addition to honours The so-called cleared-hand game. This makes going out considerably longer and wash-outs are correspondingly more frequent unless the goulash is used. The weaknesses of the cleared-hand game are that, since each player is collecting a single suit and there are only three suits, it follows that at least two players are collecting the same suit. This of course greatly diminishes their chances when compared with those of the other players. A second point is that players should be able to deduce fairly early in the game which suits the other players are collecting from their discards.

Only one chow is permitted in a mahjong hand This is an old idea with some merit as it allows more than one suit to be collected whilst at the same time limiting the prospects of a quick mahjong.

A mahjong hand must contain one double This has the same effect as the cleared-hand and is arguably more in keeping with the spirit of the game.

All chows are disallowed This is a drastic limitation running directly counter to the spirit and play of the old game. It must be compensated for by the introduction of a number of new special hands in addition to those already honoured.

Only the player going mahjong is paid The disadvantage of this restriction is that players who build powerful hands get no reward if they do not go out. A common corollary of the rule is that the discarder of a winning tile alone pays, or pays double, or also pays for the other losers.

The modern Chinese game

Whilst the older generation of Chinese may continue to play to the old rules, a younger generation has endorsed change, if anything moving closer to the American concept. The fundamentals are simpler scoring together with the expansion of nominated hands.

The scoring system is based on **Faans** and **Laaks**. Faans can be broadly compared with the doubles of the old game and laaks with limit hands. Complex scoring and settlement is reduced to grouping all mahjong hands into just four categories attracting payment of from one to four faans respectively. This is known as the 2–2 system (there is also an advanced 3–3 system) so called because an all-pung hand and a mixed hand (one suit and honours) score two faans.

A hand that fails to earn even one faan is called a chicken woo.

A chicken woo hand consists of kongs, pungs and chows of suit tiles at random, excluding sets of dragons, own wind or prevailing wind. Here is a chicken woo hand:

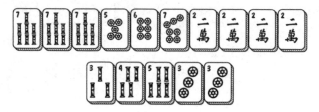

1-faan hand

Certain hands are designated 1-faan. One such is an all-chow hand, for example:

2-faan hand

This is an 'all-pung' hand. Kongs are reckoned the same as pungs. The wind is not the wind of the round or the wind of the seat:

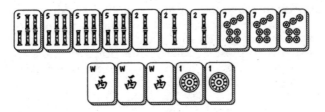

3-faan hand

A concealed 2-faan hand rates three faans. Here is an exposed 3-faan hand where South is the prevailing wind and West the player's wind:

4-faan hand

Sets and a pair of one suit only without honours:

In addition to the number of faans awarded for the hand, there are several supplementary faans that can be earned. For example, drawing the winning tile from the wall earns an extra faan, as does robbing the kong. A step beyond the faan system is the laak system.

A laak is a limit hand, equal to four or more faans, as agreed by the players. Two laaks may equate to five or six faans, three laaks to six or eight faans, again, as agreed beforehand. This system encourages players to go for big hands.

Coupled with the faan/laak system is the introduction to the game of patterns — the so-called New Style game. The New Style abandons the free hands of the old game in favour of special hands similar to those popular in America. Patterns are agreed before play and may be increased with experience. These can earn between one faan and the limit agreed. Forty such patterns are commonplace and there are some 50 others, any of which players may add to their repertoire.

Taiwanese mahjong

Hands and play are similar to the old Chinese game except that players are dealt 16 tiles (4 × 4) initially and a mahjong hand consists of five sets and a pair. Bonus tiles (flowers and seasons) are used, but no jokers. The last 16 tiles of the live wall are not used. Scoring is similar to the faan system. Only the winner is paid. If the winning tile is drawn from the wall, all players pay; if from a discard, only the discarder pays.

Mahjong in South-East Asia

The game became very popular in the region during the 1920s with each country later developing national characteristics. In particular, the use of bonus tiles and jokers has proliferated. The game in Vietnam can include many bonus tiles with sets of four

Empresses and Emperors and 'Almighty' tiles (jokers). Other bonus tiles, again in sets of four comparable to the flowers and seasons of the old game, are bundle, wan, circle, string and flower, unit, joy, money.

Thai sets are often composed of as many as 168 tiles, the basic set with no fewer than 32 bonus and joker tiles of one sort or another.

One common set of extra tiles comprises predators and victims; this is also found in sets sold in America and elsewhere. This set of four is made up of cat and rat, chicken and centipede (or sometimes old man and pot of gold or fisherman and fish). The owner of the second-named of each pair has to be careful. If the tile is declared and another player has the predator, bad luck. If, however, the predator is played first the victim can be safely exposed. These declarations are normally left until late in the game for obvious reasons but if a player is caught with any of these tiles in hand at the end of the game, there is a points penalty.

In Malaysian mahjong, as in Thai mahjong, a proliferation of bonus tiles is commonplace. Here the sets tend to be harp, xiangqi (Chinese chess), writing and painting (loosely, the arts) or fishing, logging, cultivating and reading. A three-player set marketed in Malaysia has only one suit (circles), winds, dragons, flowers, seasons and eight jokers.

Oddities

Unfamiliar tiles, not mentioned above, are found in some sets. They are almost always jokers of some sort. All that can be said of these strangers is that rules governing their use will almost certainly be included with the sets of which they are part.

13

mahjong cards

In this chapter you will learn:
- how to play the game with cards
- about different card designs.

Mahjong was almost certainly first played with cards before someone had the bright idea of transferring the game to tiles.

Until recently, **mahjong cards**, known as paper mahjong, were usually strips of paper crudely printed with stylized illustrations and ideograms by way of identification, although some packs had more elaborate coloured designs. These cards were similar in size and shape to domino cards, some of which understandably carry the same values as mahjong tallies, like those shown below:

Chinese domino cards

Today, mahjong cards can be purchased printed in full colour on quality card with the usual symbols in place of ideograms, making identification simple. Here are a few examples:

modern mahjong cards

Packs of cards roughly similar in size to ordinary playing cards and no doubt aimed primarily at the Western market, are also available. A few examples are illustrated.

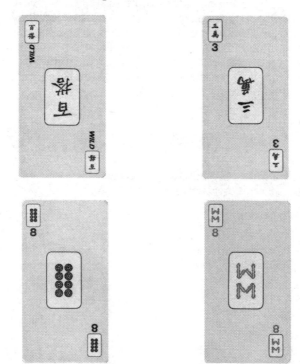

modern mahjong playing cards

The cards accompanying Derek Walter's book on divination using mahjong tiles (*The Fortune Teller's Mah Jongg* – see Further Reading section) depict delightful images of a traditional China. Here are a few of these:

mahjong divination cards
(reproduction courtesy Eddison-Sadd editions)

Playing the game with cards poses no real problems. A pack of mahjong cards usually numbers 144, including flowers and seasons, corresponding to the tiles in a standard mahjong set.

The cards are shuffled and dealt, starting and ending with the dealer (East), who thus has an extra card (14 against 13 for the other players). The remainder of the pack is stacked face down in the centre of the table. This represents the wall. If desired, the bottom 14 cards can be extracted and set aside unseen in simulation of the Chinese practice of pronouncing the last 14 tiles of the wall to be dead.

Replacement cards for bonus tiles and kongs are taken off the top of the stack in the same manner that cards are drawn normally. Discards should be placed face-up in front of each player, overlapping from right to left so that all cards are visible and are in the order in which they were discarded. In all other respects the game is mahjong.

Despite their modest cost, mahjong cards are not popular for several reasons, in particular perhaps because they lack the aural appeal of the tiles.

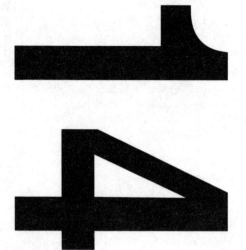

14

history

In this chapter you will learn:
- the origins of the game
- predecessors of mahjong
- the great mahjong boom
- superstitions.

Origins

The history of a game helps us towards a better understanding of it and in turn adds pleasure to the play. But history can also be, as it is with mahjong, a fascinating narrative in its own right.

The origins of mahjong, like those of most traditional games that have no known inventor, are obscure. Inevitably, there has been the temptation for some writers to accord these games long and distinguished pedigrees. In the case of mahjong this has been taken to extreme lengths. Top marks for absurdity are given to the oft-repeated story that it was played in the Ark to while away the 40 days and nights of rain. The main argument for this seems to be that at the time of the Flood an east wind prevailed and East is the dominant wind in mahjong. A refutation, if such is needed, is that the Ark had only one small window, according to the scriptures, so no-one could have seen the tiles anyway. Other claims, almost as absurd, talk of '3,000 years old', 'first recorded 500 BC', this last date inevitably linking Confucius to the game. The three dragons are said to correspond to the Confucian virtues of benevolence, sincerity and filial piety, whilst the eight bonus tiles (flowers) are sometimes known as the Guardians, and have been linked to the Eight Immortals of Chinese legend and also to the eight trinomes of the I-Ching.

There is another legend, often repeated though equally lacking in credibility, that the game was invented by a man called Sze and his nine brothers to prevent fishermen getting seasick. Less ambitious commentators have been content with statements like 'for centuries the favourite game of the Chinese'. The actress Sybil Thorndike, writing in 1924 when she was Honorary President of The Mah Jongg League, archly declared 'it is such a thrill to feel that we (the League) shall be playing in the exact way that all those fascinating Chinese have played for such centuries'.

The truth is much less dramatic. Mahjong is a recent addition to the ranks of traditional games. No firm reference to mahjong in Chinese literature or in records anywhere has been found that pre-dates the start of the twentieth century, making it extremely unlikely that the game, if it existed earlier, had achieved any measure of popularity before this time. Equally, no mahjong set or tiles have been recorded before 1880. And that identification is by no means conclusive and does not constitute proof of the existence of the game as we know it, because as many games can be played with a set of mahjong tiles as can be played with a pack of playing cards. It is true, however, that the games from which mahjong was undoubtedly developed go far back into the past. China has a long tradition of dice, domino (tile) and card games associated with gambling that can be traced back many centuries. Chinese playing cards are traditionally slim slips of waxed paper or similar, often crudely printed. It was foreigners, however, who were the first to attempt research into the subject.

A British consular official, William Wilkinson, whose post gave him the opportunity to travel within China, collected packs of Chinese playing cards over a five-year period towards the end of the nineteenth century. He sent 45 of these packs to Stewart Culin in America for display at the Columbian Exposition in Chicago. They are now housed in the Pennsylvania University Museum. Culin was an authority on oriental games and it is perhaps significant that in his book on Chinese games (1895) no mention is made of mahjong.

Wilkinson presented another 34 packs of playing cards to Lady Charlotte Schreiber, who subsequently bequeathed them, together with her own collection, to the British Museum. None of these 79 packs can be firmly identified as mahjong cards. Collectively they fall into four groups. Millington gives these as dominoes (which in turn are derived from dice), xiangqi (the Chinese form of chess), literary (aphorisms and sayings) and money-related. Only the first and in particular the last group concern us. There appears always to have been a cross-fertilization between dice, domino and card games in China (the word pai in Chinese can mean any of these which does not make the researcher's task easy). As an example of the inter-relationship, one domino game, K'ap t'ai shap, that pre-dates mahjong, requires walls to be built whilst a winning hand consists of four sets of number-related dominoes and an identical pair. In another old game, T'ien Chui (Heavens and Nines), the leader, like East in mahjong, pays or receives double in settlements. Chinese dominoes differ from those in the West being composed of two sets, civil and military, totalling 32 tiles.

It is the money cards, however, that demonstrate the closest links to mahjong. Paper money originated in China as far back as the eleventh century and cards printed with sums of money became popular soon afterwards. Their appeal endured: Chinese who had little or no money — doubtless the vast majority of the population — could derive a vicarious sense of wealth playing with them. With few exceptions the rules of these games are unrecorded so the best we can do is hazard guesses as to how they were played. Mahjong almost certainly evolved from an amalgam of these games and in particular set-forming card games, such as had been played all over China since at least the seventeenth century and probably much earlier. Cards is perhaps a loose term in this context since, although commonly of pasteboard, crudely printed with ideographs, the same packs were also sometimes manufactured in more durable material, such as wood or bone.

Two card games in particular, both popular in nineteenth-century China and both depicting Ming dynasty banknotes, have strong claims to be the forerunners of mahjong. The game most closely associated with mahjong is **Ma-Tiao** (**Hanging Horse**), which may have been played as early as the fifteenth century and was certainly current by the seventeenth century. The game was played with 40 cards made up of four suits numbered from 1 to 9 (one card of each value) decorated with fictional characters, together with four bonus cards, comparable to the flower and season cards of modern mahjong. This 40-card pack was later expanded to 108 cards, with the four suits reduced to three suits, numbered 1 to 9, with four tiles of each value thus corresponding in number to the tiles of the three mahjong suits. The cards often bore representations of brigands from a classical Chinese novel of the period *Shui Hu Chuan* (Story of the River Bank).

Ma-Tiao, according to some researchers, is derived from an earlier card game, Ya-pai, itself the development of an even earlier game, Yeh-tzu-pai. These money-derived suits were **cash**, **strings** and **myriads**. Cash were small copper coins with a hole in the centre, a basic currency of Imperial China. Cash can be equated to the circle suit. It was the practice of the poorer elements of society at the time to thread the coins on strings, knotted at intervals to facilitate counting. Strings were classified in Ma-Tiao as 1000 cash (other card games had suits representing tens and hundreds of cash). It does not require much imagination to see how these strings were stylized into strips of bamboo that would have wider commercial appeal, particularly for a game aimed at overseas markets. Myriads (ten-thousands), called **wan** or **won**, translate exactly to the won of the character suit. The parallels between Ma-Tiao and mahjong are so obvious that it would be foolish to deny the influence of the former on the latter.

The second card game that appears to have strong links with mahjong is **K'an Hu** (**Watch-the-pot**), a game that is alleged to go as far back as the twelfth century. K'an Hu had the usual money suits plus three additional cards, **Redflower**, **Whiteflower** and **Old Thousand**. Again, little imagination is required to see these as precursors of the three dragons. We find in K'an Hu other parallels with mahjong. For instance, the first player is dealt an extra card and starts by discarding; and a player can 'pung' to claim a discard to complete a set of three. A player claiming a discard must then himself discard when play moves to the right. The game was often played with five jokers known as Golds (so called because they were originally distinguished by a blob of gilt), corresponding to the five celestial blessings, long life, peace, promotion, posterity and wealth.

K'an Hu (described in promotional material as 'universally popular') was introduced into Britain by W. H. Wilkinson as **Khanhoo** and was first described in a book of that name published in 1891. The game was adapted for the English market by naming the three suits, each with cards numbered ace to nine, as hearts, clubs and diamonds with a neutral king, queen, jack (corresponding, apparently, to Redflower, Whiteflower and Old Thousand) and a joker, making a pack of 31 cards. K'an Hu, according to Wilkinson, was one of the two national card games of China with the unique distinction for a card game of being equally good for two, three or four players.

Money-derived playing cards from a Beijing pack (late nineteenth century) in the Schreiber collection clearly illustrate the relationship between card games of the period and mahjong.

examples from a pack of money-based cards (late nineteenth century)
(Schreiber collection; courtesy of the British Museum)

Here the link to mahjong is clear. From left to right there are four cash (circle) cards, a flower (bonus) card, two ligatures (bamboos) and five character cards respectively numbered 8, 2, 6, 9 and 4. Character cards commonly bore portraits representing some story or historical figures but these were understandably dropped when the designs were transferred to tiles. The winds and dragons were later additions to the game, as were probably the flowers and seasons. One suspects that these tiles were introduced partly for their aesthetic appeal and hence for their commercial value.

Mahjong as we know it is believed to have started life in East Central China in the area around Shanghai. The former treaty port of **Ningbo**, first visited by the Portuguese in the sixteenth century, has been identified as a possible birthplace, in part because one or two of the game's terms are in the Ningbo dialect, but this must remain largely conjecture. What is not in dispute is that the game spread quickly all over China. Understandably, a game that is passed largely by word of mouth suffers changes, if only minor ones. South and North China had their own versions of the game and at regional level rule differences were recorded in Canton, Fukien, Shanghai, Soochow and elsewhere. Mahjong in Chinese has a dual ideogram but almost as many names as there are dialects in the country: Ma Cheuk (Cantonese), Ma Chang, Ma Ch'iau, Majiang, Pung Chow, Pe-ling and Lung Chan to quote a few.

Elisabeth Papineau has described mahjong with good reason as 'the fruit of an astonishing series of metamorphoses'. Card games, because of their identification with gambling, have been banned from time to time. Card playing was one of the 'four vices' under the Ming dynasty; and later under the communists mahjong was demonized as one of the 'four olds'. During the cultural revolution the game was commonly played with cards as the tell-tale clacking of tiles could be overheard and reported. In mockery of the government and party exhortations that abounded at the time, resistance was expressed in the slogan 'study edict 144' referring to the 144 tiles of the game. In China, where men and women play the game separately, the 'new mahjong' came into being after World War II. Its hallmark is the scoring system described in Chapter 12. It is now well established in Hong Kong and in countries like Singapore.

Mahjong had never had a national organization in the country of its birth until very recently when the authorities, in an effort to control and promote the game of 'healthy mahjong' (i.e. no gambling), caused the Athletics Council of the Chinese Government to declare mahjong a sport and a definitive *Rules of Chinese Mahjong* was published in 1998.

The rules cover 81 different hands (combinations), each one scoring between one and 88 points. The top-scoring hands include Four Large Blessings, Gates of Heaven, Thirteen Unique Wonders, Imperial Jade, Fourfold Plenty and Three Great Scholars (described above, pp. 58–62). These rules are in force for the World Championship for National Teams and are published by Take Shobo Co. as *The World Rule of Mahjong*.

The slang names coined for certain tiles in the West have their parallels in contemporary China. According to one source, the sobriquets for the Circle suit are:

1 of circles — pancake
2 of circles — spectacles
3 of circles — counterfeit money
4 of circles — automobile
5 of circles — tortoise or cuckold
6 of circles — stepmother
7 of circles — fireplace
8 of circles — old pig
9 of circles — marijuana

In the early years of the twentieth century mahjong was played with enthusiasm in the expatriate circles of Shanghai, such as the Union and the American Clubs. It is here that the numbering of character tiles and later of the other two suits together with the letter indices identifying the winds were probably introduced for the benefit of foreigners. Sets intended for the local market understandably carried no indices.

The great mahjong boom

An American, Joseph Babcock, who patented the name mah-jongg in America (the name Ma Chiang had been patented in Britain as far back as 1912), is credited with first introducing mahjong to the West when he set about promoting the game in America around 1920. Here mahjong saw a cycle of change and experiment, and to talk of one particular game as American mahjong was as inaccurate during the 1920s as it is today. The subsequent craze for the game that swept the United States, where it still commands a large following, Britain and much of

Europe is unparalleled in the history of table games. A large number of instructional books were published in the early- to mid-1920s, capitalizing on the new craze.

Decline then set in. It can be attributed to two factors: the proliferation of rules and special hands that invaded and corrupted the classical version leading to a diminished interest in the game, and the rise of Contract Bridge. Since that time mahjong has enjoyed periods of popularity in both America and, less enthusiastically, in Europe, although never anything approaching that of the boom years.

Mahjong found its way to Japan in the early years of the twentieth century and eventually became immensely popular. Today, the world's strongest players are to be found there. The Mahjong Museum, at Misaki-cho near Tokyo, — the only one in the world — was opened in 1999. It has an awe-inspiring collection of sets, including one previously owned by the last emperor of China, Pu-yi (illustrated).

the set belonging to Pu-yi, the last Emperor of China
(courtesy the Mahjong Museum)

From the earliest years of the twentieth century up to about 1930 mahjong tiles were hand-made and engraved, which accounts for their seemingly endless diversity of design and in many cases for their beauty. In the years immediately following World War I workshops and small factories sprang up in

Shanghai and elsewhere to meet the huge demands for sets from overseas. Usually an individual workman had one particular task and a tile would be passed from one artisan to another and from one shop to another before completion. Western enterprise then stepped in, building a large factory near Shanghai that employed some 400 highly skilled workers. Mahjong sets rapidly became one of the major exports from the province.

Mahjong has its forerunners and variants like all popular board and table games. One of these is Ma-tchiao-pai, which has the three suits and four winds together with five 'superior' tiles: the centre, prosperity, the phoenix, the dragon, and white, the last three clearly the three dragons of mahjong. Another game, popular in Malaysia, is Sap-tim-pun (Ten-&-a-half), played with mahjong tiles.

Superstitions

Unsurprisingly, superstition has invaded the game. It is good luck, for example, to complete your wall before the other players and also to hit the opposite tile wall when casting the dice, but beware! If the dice jump the wall and land on the floor that is a bad omen. During the deal it is lucky to draw the four tiles from the corner of a wall as according to tradition these will invariably include a dragon, prevailing wind or own wind. When you are on a winning streak never change your chair or wash your hands. As East wind, put the dice in front of you so that they total 5 or 9 (indicating East) and if when you roll them they sum to 5 or 9, good fortune is yours. If you are having a run of bad luck, get up and walk round your chair, while if you wish to bring bad luck on another player, pick up his discard or wall tile for him. It is also very bad luck, although it is not clear to whom, if East wind discards a west wind tile and the other three players all discard west winds, not, fortunately, a very likely occurrence.

Mahjong also lends itself to philosophy, symbolism, and to divination and writers have not been slow to take advantage of this. Nor is numerology neglected. The number 144 (the number of tiles in a set, including bonus tiles) is uniquely linked with the number 216 in the harmonious relationship of yin and yang, of the square earth and the round sky. There is one certainty: mahjong, in its many reincarnations, will be with us for a long, long time.

Further reading

The following books, dating from the boom years of the game, are all out of print and mostly rare, but copies can be found in some major public libraries. Recommended are *Mahjong Simplified* (Henry Peterson), which includes the Queens' Club rules, *Standardized Mahjong* (Lee F. Hartman), which includes the American Official Laws of Mah-Jongg (1924) drafted by Hartman and others, and *Hints on Skill & Tactics of Playing Mahjongg* (Olga Racster).

Rules for Mahjong (unattributed, 1920)
Ma Chang by Harold Sterling (Harold Carey) (1921)
Ma-cheuk by Roger E. Lindsell (1922)
Mahjong's Do's and Don'ts by Eileen Beck (1923)
How to Play Mah-jong by Jean Bray (1923)
Mahjong & How to Play It by Etienne (1923)
How to Play Pung Chow by L. L. Harr (1923)
Mahjongg by East Wind (1923)
The Laws of Mahjong by Robert F. Foster (1923)
Foster's Mahjong Scorecard by Robert F. Foster (1923)
Babcock's Rules for Mahjong by Joseph Babcock (1923)
Pocket Guide to Mahjong (unattributed, 1923)
Ma Cheuk as Played by the Chinese by Edgar S. Winters (1923)
Mahjong in Plain English by Tei-Tei Woo (1923)
Mahjong & How to Play It by Chiang Lee (1923)
Sparrow, the Chinese Game Called Ma-Ch'iau by Ly Yu Sang (1923)
Snyder's Mah Jong Manual by Henry Snyder (1923)
Mah Jong by East Wind (1923)
Mah-Jongg, Sometimes called Sparrow (Chad Valley, 1923)
The Pocket Guide to Mah Jong (De la Rue, 1924)

The Game of Ma Chiang by Prescott Warren (E. S. Warren) (1924)

The Outline of Mahjong by Julius S. Tow (1924)

Foster's 20-point Mahjong Scorecard by Robert F. Foster (1924)

Twenty-point Mahjong by Robert F. Foster (1924)

Standardized Mahjong by Lee F. Hartman (1924)

Directions for Playing Ma Jong by L. Ranger (1924)

Mahjong Rules of the Queens' Club (1924)

The Complete Mah Jong Player by Florence Irwin (1924)

Mahjong Simplified by Henry Peterson (1924)

Foster on Mahjong by Robert F. Foster (1924)

25 Mahjongg Limit Hands & Hints by Green Dragon (1924)

Mahjongg — How to Play and Score by C. M. W. Higginson (1924)

International Mahjong (unattributed, 1924)

Hints on Skill & Tactics of Playing Mahjongg by Olga Racster (1924)

Official Rules of the Mahjongg League by Olga Racster (1924)

American Code of Laws of Mahjong (1924)

The Theory of Mahjong by Wei (1925)

The Mastering of Mahjong by Tei-Tei Teng (1925)

Mah-Jongg Up-to-Date by Milton C. Work (1925)

The Laws of Mahjong by Joseph Babcock (1925)

Several of the following books are still in print. The date, where given, is of the first edition. The publisher quoted is not necessarily the publisher of the first edition. Strongly recommended is the authoritative book on the Chinese game, *The Complete Book of Mah-jongg* by A. D. Millington. Recommended is *A Mah Jong Handbook*, primarily on the Japanese game, by Eleanor Noss Whitney.

Chinese Game of Four Winds (unattributed/undated)

Mah-jong Made Easy by Esmond Talbot (1933)

The Game of Mah Jong by Max Robertson (Whitcombe & Tombs, 1938)

Modern Mahjong by T. Lane (1938)

Mahjong the Chinese Way by K. S. Whitehead (1943)

Mah Jong for Beginners by Shozo Kanai & Margaret Farrell (Tuttle, 1955)

A Mah Jong Handbook by Eleanor Noss Whitney (Tuttle, 1964)

Mah Jong Anyone? by Kitty Strauser and Lucille Evans (Charles Tuttle, 1964)

Discovering Mah-jong by Robert C. Bell (Shire Publications, 1976)

The Complete Book of Mah-jongg by A. D. Millington (Arthur Barker, 1977)

Know the Game Mah-Jong by Gwyn Headley and Yvonne Seeley (A. & C. Black, 1978)

The Chinese Game of Mahjong by S. K. Perleman and & Mark Chan (Book Marketing Ltd, 1979)

Learn to Play Mah Jongg: From Beginner to Winner by Marcia Hammer (D. McKay Co., 1979)

Basic Mahjong by Lewis Ting (Times Books, 1981)

The Game of Mah Jong by Patricia Thompson and Betty Maloney (Kangaroo Press, 1990)

Let's Play Mahjong! by Benny Constantino (Federal Publications Hong Kong, 1990)

Improve Your Mah Jong by Patricia Thompson and Betty Maloney (Kangaroo Press, 1991)

How to Play Mah Jong by K. J. Carkner (Penguin Books Australia, 1993)

Your Future Revealed by the Mah Jongg by Derek Walters (Aquarian Press, 1982)

The Fortune Teller's Mah Jongg by Derek Walters (Michael Joseph, 1988)

The Mah Jong Player's Companion by Patricia Thompson and Betty Maloney (Kangaroo Press, 1997)

Mahjong Basic Rules and Strategy by Dieter Kohnen (Sterling Publications, 1998)

The Happy Game of Mah-Jong by David H. Li (Premier Publishing, 1999)

Mah-Jong The illustrated book of the mahjong museum, Tokyo (2000)

Rules, etc.

Mah Jongg Made Easy National Mah Jongg League (1984)

International Mahjong Rules by Cofa Tsui (1998) International Mah Jong website

Mah-Jongg: Wright-Patterson rules (1963–1996) Wright-Patterson Mah Jongg Group

The World Rule of Mahjong (Take Shobo Co., 2000). The address of the publishers is on p.115

In French

Le Mah-jong by P. Berger and J.-M. Etienne (L'Impensé Radicale, 1986)

Traité du jeu de mah-jong by P. Berger and J.-M. Etienne (Chiron, 1994)

Le Livre du Mahjong by P. Reysset and T. Depaulis (Bornemann, 1996)

Le jeu dans la Chine Contemporaine by Elisabeth Papineau (L'Harmattan, 2000)

Websites

There are a number of websites devoted to mahjong. Here are a few:

www.mahjongnews.com
www.mahjongg.com
www.ninedragons.com
http://mahjong.real-time.com/

Acknowledgements

The cards on page 124 are copyright © Eddison Sadd Editions 1988. They are illustrated by Amanda Barlow and selected from *The Fortune Teller's Mah Jong* by Derek Walters, published by Connections Book Publishing, and reproduced from Eddison Sadd Editions.

glossary

Accessories Useful aids for play but not essential for the game. These include racks, tallies, wind discs and rulers.

All Honours Hand of all honour tiles (dragons and winds) only.

All Pair Honours Mixed hand of seven pairs of terminals and honours.

All Pairs Hand consisting of pairs of tiles of one suit plus pairs of dragons/winds in any combination.

Autumn Bonus tile proper to West.

Babcock, Joseph American resident of Shanghai who introduced mahjong to the United States.

Bamboo Bonus tile proper to North. A tile of the bamboo suit.

Bamboos One of the three suits in a mahjong set.

Bams Popular American term for bamboos.

Bones A popular name for tallies.

Bonus tiles The flowers and seasons.

Bouquet A set of four flowers or seasons.

Buried Treasure Hand of four concealed pungs and any pair, last tile drawn from the wall.

Calling Player requiring one tile to go mahjong. Fishing, waiting, ready.

Cannon, Letting off a Discarding a tile evidently required by a calling player for certain mahjong hands.

Cards Mahjong cards; a term sometimes used for tiles.

Cash Copper coins, the origin of the circles suit.

Catching the Moon from the Bottom of the Sea Going out with a 1 of circles if last tile on the live wall.

Characters One of the three suits in a mahjong set.

Charleston System widely adopted in America in which tiles are exchanged between players before the game starts.

Chips Tallies or bones used in payment.

Chow   Three suit tiles in sequence, a run.

Chrysanthemum   Bonus tile proper to West.

Chuang-tzu   The jong box, container for wind discs.

Circles   One of the three suits in a mahjong set.

Clean Pairs   Hand of pairs (one suit) and honours.

Cleared Hand   A hand containing one suit only with or without honours or a hand of honours and/or terminals only.

Concealed   Tiles hidden from the other players.

Courtyard   Space between the walls where tiles are discarded.

Cracks   An American name for characters.

Craks   An alternative spelling of cracks.

Deal   Initial distribution of tiles from the wall.

Dealer   Player occupying the East seat, the leader.

Dirty Pairs   Hand of seven pairs of any tiles.

Discard   Tile played face up to the table.

Discard, sacred   Tile required to go out identical to one player has previously discarded (Japanese mahjong); fu.

Discs   Wind discs, usually contained in a jong box

Dots   Name, common in America, for the circle suit.

Double   Set, hand or situation that permits a player to double his score.

Dragonet   Hand of three pairs in one suit, pair of honours, six odd honours.

Dragonfly   Hand of three pungs (three suits), one of each dragon, any pair of suit tiles.

Dragons   Honour tiles. There are three dragons: red, green and white.

Dragons, Big Three   Hand of three sets of dragons.

Dragon's Breath   Hand of five pairs (one suit), one of each dragon, one paired.

Dragon's Tail   Hand of 1–9 (one suit), set of dragons and pair of winds or set of winds and pair of dragons.

Draw   Situation where the live wall is exhausted and no player has gone mahjong. A wash-out.

Earth's Blessing   Mahjong hand completed by claiming East's first discard.

Exposed   Set of tiles placed face up to indicate it has been formed from a discard; a bonus tile so placed.

Eyes   Pair in mahjong hand; pillow. Short for Eyes of the bird.

Faan   Unit of scoring in modern Chinese game, equivalent to a double.

False declaration   An invalid claim.

Fishing   Player calling for a tile identical to one held in order to go mahjong; sometimes used in the general sense of calling or waiting.

Five Odd Honours   Hand of 1–9 (one suit) and five odd honours.

Flower, own   Flower tile that corresponds to the player's seat.

Flowers   Set of bonus tiles; collectively suits of flowers and seasons.

Fourfold Plenty   Limit hand containing four kongs and any pair.

Four Joys in Full   Hand of four sets of winds and any pair.

Four Large Blessings   Same hand as Four Joys in Full.

Four Smaller Blessings   Hand of three sets of winds, any pung and a pair.

Fu   Sacred discard (Japanese mahjong).

Game   Four rounds of play; a minimum of 16 hands.

Gates of Heaven   Concealed one-suit hand composed of three of each of the terminals and a run of 2–8 with any tile doubled; Nine Gates.

Gathering Plum Blossom from the Roof   Limit hand in which a 5 of circles is drawn from the kong box.

Gertie's Garter   Pairs hand of 1–7 in each of two suits.

Goulash   Charleston; the exchange of tiles between players before start of play with the aim of improving hands.

Great Wall of China   The walls of tiles when pushed together.

Green tiles   The 2, 3, 4, 6 and 8 of bamboos and the green dragon.

Greta's Garden   Hand of 1–7 in one suit, one each of dragons and winds.

Hand   A single deal, ending in mahjong or a wash-out; a player's tile holding.

Hand, dead   Hand with too many or too few tiles making mahjong impossible. An impure hand.

Hand, impure   Hand that contains an incorrect number of tiles. Dead hand.

Hand, long   Hand that contains too many tiles.

Hand, mixed   Hand that contains tiles of more than one suit.

Hand, pure   Hand that contains correct number of tiles.

Hand, short   Hand that contains too few tiles.

Hanging Horse   Ma-tiao; Chinese card game believed to be one of the predecessors of mahjong.

Heads and Tails   Hand composed entirely of terminals.

Heaven's Blessing   East goes out on his first turn without discarding.

Heavenly Twins   Hand of seven pairs of tiles (one suit).

Honour tiles   Dragons and winds.

Imperial Jade   A hand composed entirely of green tiles.

Isolated tile   A tile that has no link to any other tile in a hand.

Joker   A tile that can be substituted for any tile.

Jong The occupier of the East seat.

Jong box The chuang-tzu; container for wind discs.

K'an Hu Watch-the-Pot; Chinese card game believed to be one of the predecessors of mahjong.

Khanhoo A commercial version of K'an Hu marketed in the U.K. at the start of the twentieth century.

Knitting Hand of seven pairs (two suits only).

Kong A set of four identical tiles.

Kong Box The dead wall from which replacements for kongs and bonus tiles are drawn.

Kong on Kong Replacement tile for kong completes second kong whose replacement completes mahjong; a limit hand.

Laak Unit of scoring in modern Chinese game, roughly equivalent to a limit.

Leader The occupier of the East seat.

Limit Maximum number of points that can be won on a single hand.

Limit hand Hand that earns the limit.

Loose tiles The tiles on top of the dead wall.

Lucky thirteen East goes mahjong 13 consecutive times.

Lucky tile A dragon, prevailing wind or own wind tile (American).

Ma-tiao Hanging Horse; a Chinese card game believed to be one of the predecessors of mahjong.

Mahjong A hand composed of four sets and a pair. A mahjong hand can vary between 14 and 18 tiles.

Mahjong cards Playing cards that substitute for tiles.

Meld A set; to complete a set.

Mixed-hand game Game in which mixed suits are permitted.

Myriad Ten thousand; wan or won; forerunner of characters suit.

Natural winning Same as Heaven's Blessing.

Nine Gates Gates of Heaven.

Ningbo A city near to Shanghai believed by some to be the birthplace of mahjong.

Old Thousand A card in K'an Hu, possibly a forerunner of the green dragon.

One-double game A game, especially in America, that requires a player's hand to qualify for at least one double before going mahjong.

Orchid Bonus tile proper to South.

Original Call Calling hand announced by a player after that player's first discard.

Own flower The flower tile that corresponds to the player's seat.

Own season   The season tile that corresponds to the player's seat.

Own wind   The wind that corresponds to the player's seat.

Pair   Two identical tiles; the pair of tiles necessary to complete a mahjong hand.

Penalties   Impositions for infringements of the rules.

Pillow   Pair of identical tiles in a mahjong hand; Head of the sparrow, Eyes of the bird.

Plum blossom   Bonus tile proper to East.

Points   The basic units of the scoring system.

Prevailing wind   The wind of the round.

Provisional East   Player who rolls the dice initially to determine who will be East.

Pung   A set of three identical tiles, a triplet.

Purity   Hand of four pungs/kongs and a pair (one suit).

Quint   A set of five identical tiles (American mahjong).

Razzle   Another name for the Charleston.

Ready   A player requiring one tile for mahjong (Japanese mahjong). Calling, fishing, waiting.

Redflower   Card in K'an Hu, possible forerunner of the red dragon.

Riichi   Ready (Japanese mahjong).

Round   A series of hands in which each player in turn is designated East.

Royal Ruby   Hand of pungs of red bamboos/red dragons.

Ruby Jade   Hand of sets of red and green dragons, one set each red and green bamboos, any bamboo pair.

Ruby Hand   Hand of seven pairs of red bamboos/red dragons.

Run   A chow.

Score   Total points earned at the end of a hand.

Scratching a Carrying Pole   Robbing a kong of 2 bamboos.

Season, own   Season tile that corresponds to the player's seat.

Seasons   Set of bonus tiles.

Self-drawn   A tile drawn from the wall.

Sequence   Suit tiles in successive order; chow, run.

Settlement   Payments made by the players at the end of a hand.

Set   A chow, pung or kong; the pair that completes a mahjong hand.

Shuffle   The initial mixing of the tiles face down; washing.

Simple   Any suit tile between 2 and 8 inclusive.

Sparrow, Head of the   Pair of identical tiles in a mahjong hand; Eyes of the bird, pillow.

Sparrows, Twittering of the   Washing. Term given to initial shuffling of the tiles.

Spring   Bonus tile proper to East.

Stack   Two tiles, one on top of the other.

Standing Hand   Same as Original Call.

String   1000 cash; forerunner of bamboos

Suit   Any one of three sets of tiles numbered from 1 to 9.

Summer   Bonus tile proper to South.

Tallies   Bones or counters used in settlements.

Terminals   The 1s and 9s of each of the three suits.

Thirteen Grades of Imperial Treasure   Same hand as Thirteen Unique Wonders.

Thirteen Unique Wonders   Limit hand; one each of terminals, dragons and winds, any one paired

Three Great Scholars   Hand of three sets of dragons, any pung or kong and any pair.

Three Lesser Scholars   Hand including two sets of dragons and a pair of the third.

Tile, Honour   The winds and the dragons.

Tile, Lucky   A dragon tile, a wind of the round or a player's own wind (American mahjong).

Tile, Major   An honour tile or a terminal.

Tile, Minor   Any suit tile 2–8 inclusive.

Tiles, green   The green dragon and 2, 3, 4, 6 and 8 of bamboos.

Tiles, red   The red dragon and 1, 5, 7 and 9 of bamboos.

Tiles, supplementary   Tiles over and above the standard set of 136 and the bonus tiles.

Triple Knitting   Four triplets (same value in three suits), pair (two suits).

Triplet   Three of a kind, a pung; three tiles of same value in three suits.

Unnatural winning   Same as Earth's Blessing.

Waiting   A player who needs one tile for mahjong; calling, ready, fishing.

Wall   Initial arrangement of tiles.

Wall, dead   The kong box; the 16 tiles set aside to provide replacements for kongs and bonus tiles.

Wall, live   That part of the wall from which the players draw tiles during play.

Wan   Ten-thousand; the symbol for the character suit.

Wash-out   A draw; the situation when no player has gone out and the live wall is exhausted.

Washing   Initial shuffling of the tiles; twittering of the sparrows.

Watch-the-pot   K'an hu; Chinese card game believed to be one of the predecessors of mahjong.

Whiteflower   Card in K'an hu, possible forerunner of white dragon.

Wind Disc A plastic disc rotated to reveal the wind of the round.

Windfall Hand of five pairs (one suit), one of each wind.

Wind of the round Prevailing wind.

Wind, own Wind that corresponds to the player's seat.

Wind, prevailing Wind of the round.

Winds The 16 honour tiles; four each of East, South, West and North.

Windy Chow Hand of three chows (different suits), one of each wind, one paired.

Winter Bonus tile proper to North.

Won Ten-thousand; an alternative spelling of wan.

Woo To go mahjong.

Wriggly Snake Hand of 1–9 (one suit) one of each wind, one tile paired.

Zero Value given to the white dragon (American mahjong).

index